jump
start
$\longrightarrow$

Daniella Moyles is an author and a yoga and meditation teacher. Beginning her career aged 17, she worked primarily as a model before transitioning to television and radio presenting. In 2017 she left that decade-long career behind to backpack around the globe for a number of years. She is currently undertaking a degree to become a psychotherapist and is the founder of The STLL, a holistic-living and wellness business.

jump start →

A JOURNAL FOR ANYONE IN
SEARCH OF HAPPINESS, STRENGTH
AND AUTHENTICITY

DANIELLA MOYLES

Gill Books

Gill Books
Hume Avenue
Park West
Dublin 12
www.gillbooks.ie
Gill Books is an imprint of M.H. Gill and Co.

© Daniella Moyles 2021

9780717191093

Edited by Emma Dunne
Proofread by Jane Rogers
Designed by iota (www.iota-books.ie)
This book is typeset in Sabon
Printed by BZ Graf, Poland

The paper used in this book comes from the
wood pulp of managed forests. For every tree
felled, at least one tree is planted, thereby
renewing natural resources.

5 4 3 2 1

For my Bud, the very best guy I know. Born with all the emotional intelligence I had to work so hard to learn. Every day I am honoured and proud to be your sister. Thank you for keeping all the plates spinning while I wrote. Until the end of time, I've got your back, and I know you've got mine.

Author's note

This workbook is your beginner's guide to using cognitive behavioural therapy techniques, contemplative self-reflection, journalling and mindfulness practices for positive self-development. These are brilliant, robustly researched tools and the foundation for great change. As a trainee psychotherapist, as well as a yoga and meditation teacher, I am very passionate about their use. For some, these tools alone may be all that's required for profound self-development. However, there is a reason the field of mental health exists. These tools alone will not heal serious childhood trauma, cure a mental illness or treat serious mental health symptoms – in these cases they should be used in conjunction with the guidance of a registered, compassionate mental health professional. These tools should also not be used as a means to avoid the (often painful) work of true therapeutic emotional healing. Your mental health is one of the most important factors determining the happiness of your life and nothing can bypass or substitute for the difficult work that happens in the therapy room.

contents

introduction

'The unexamined life is not worth living'
— SOCRATES

Until the age of 29 I lived an entirely unexamined life, one which was viewed through the lens of a completely untrained mind. I was the embodiment of unconstrained desire-seeking in the absence of authentic reflection.

Aged 31, after a number of years spent circling the globe, half running away from and half searching for some answers, I wrote my memoir, *Jump*. What began as pages of private journal entries, bulleted lists and often confused rambling streams of thought eventually grew into an unintentional sort of autobiography, which depicted my very painful and unexpected unravelling into some kind of coming to consciousness. After it was published I heard from a lot of people who were shocked or moved by the story, because it had appeared I had been living a 'perfect on paper' life before it all fell apart; and when I thought about it, they were right. Even I had been stunned by my own collapse given my circumstances – I thought I'd done everything exactly as you're meant to.

If you've read *Jump* you'll be familiar with these details from what now feels like a previous life, but for those who haven't, a brief summary. By age 28, in 2017, I was a successful model, breakfast radio presenter and budding online influencer – my favourite area of influence being travel, sharing pictures and stories from many beautiful and exotic places. I was financially independent, living in a penthouse apartment, driving a brand new car and in a position to indulge in whatever material spending might take my fancy without a second thought or worry. I was also in a passionate relationship with a well-known, handsome and sought-after man, and by all outward social standards had it very much together. Maybe even desirably so.

Interestingly, what I was so sorely and blindly missing was the foundation on which this 'perfect on paper' life should have been built. To steal the words from an inspirational Instagram quote I saw recently, 'If a child can do advanced math, speak three languages or receive top grades but can't manage their emotions, practise conflict resolution or handle stress, none of that other stuff is really going to matter' – I was a grown woman with a successful career, a flourishing bank balance, a seemingly enviable relationship and a prosperous future, yet as each year passed and each prescribed milestone for happiness was met, this quote continued to ring true as my emotional, relational and spiritual deficits grew more destabilising and contentment continued to elude me. Every step I'd taken to get to that point, I'd taken in the metaphorical dark, bounced around by my whims and habits, manipulated by advertisers and marketers. My preferences were shallow – driven mostly by social and cultural pressures – and in hindsight, my major life decisions were generally based on my short-lived wanting rather than my long-term authentic values, which at that point had only been loosely established.

My instinctual compass for life: seek pleasure, avoid pain. Yet no matter how much I achieved or acquired there was always someone who had done better or amassed more. There was always an undulating undertone of unrest or agitation, a sense that real happiness awaited me somewhere in the future. Maybe you can relate to this feeling?

I am now heading for my mid-thirties and have returned to college for four years to study for my bachelor's degree in counselling and psychotherapy. I'm single, living with my parents, and have nowhere near the financial independence I had achieved a decade earlier. Assessing my current situation by those same outward social standards, I'm now very much behind, if not completely lost. But it really doesn't feel that way to me. The last number of years have afforded me a peace of mind and a sense of self I'd been unable to discover amidst all the external gains of my twenties. They have afforded me a self-assuredness around what I do *not* want, even if that goes against the grain. In leaving it all behind to start anew, I learned that there is a lot of beauty to be found in pain and loss, a lot of purpose in discomfort and a lot of freedom down the path of most resistance.

I'm also welcoming the fact that learning to observe, accept, respect, possibly alter and ultimately love oneself is a life's work, never fully realised, as we navigate the unrelenting challenges and changes that come with each passing phase of being human. But this journey can be taken in connection to a constant undercurrent of wellbeing, one that even allows us to view our adversities as opportunities for growth. In my experience, both personally and from speaking to others who work in the nuanced world of self-development, this is best achieved through the slow and repeated practice of self-awareness. This is where the space between stimulus and response is found, that unconscious link between a feeling and the behavioural imperative it seems to communicate. This is the ability to enact our free will through earned insight and presence of mind – to pause and choose our reaction or nonreaction before getting hijacked by our emotional response or our habitual behaviours. Self-awareness affords us choices that wouldn't otherwise be available to us without it, and these are paths taken and not taken in the course of one's life. If that's not reason enough to do this work, I don't know what is.

An untrained mind
– even a perfectly
normal one – can be
an extraordinarily
unhappy place

– SAM HARRIS

I have always felt that the journey I took throughout the pages of *Jump* was predominately an inner one – backdropped by the various interesting, exciting and exotic locations of the outer one, but still, at its essence, a journey one could take in their bedroom much the same. Within the pages of this journal is the work of that inner journey: the tools to examine your life, train your mind and build self-awareness – the foundation upon which all wellbeing sits and all change occurs. The tools to connect to that constant current of wellbeing, hope, positivity and joy in spite of life's guarantee of disappointment, loss and uncertainty. As we grow in mindfulness we will begin to notice the lies we can no longer tell ourselves – we will begin to have insights into our true motives in various situations, and this is not always flattering work. But we want these insights all the same because it is the best route I know to becoming the best version of yourself.

Anyone who has real experience in mental training like this will tell you that there is something to be discovered there that they were missing – and it's something that most people are still missing, without even the slightest notion that they are missing it! The fact that none of us are told this in school or by a doctor indicates nothing more than a present-day cultural blind spot – similar to the blind spot of the forties and fifties when smoking was genuinely considered a healthy habit. It shouldn't come as a surprise that we need to train our minds the same way we train our bodies. But if you require more evidence, you already know what it's like to have an untrained mind – we all do.

WHAT WILL WE EXPLORE?

Together we will work our way through the following themes, which those of you who have read *Jump* will recognise:

1. Early childhood experience and attachment theory
2. Our core psychological challenges
3. Navigating conflict
4. Managing intense emotions
5. Understanding and handling stress
6. Core personal values
7. Self-limiting beliefs and negative self-talk
8. The science of awe and gratitude
9. Love and relationships
10. Future-self journalling

HOW WILL WE EXPLORE?

No one is more of an expert on you than you, and no one can design or build the life you want better than you can. Equally, your mind is *all* you have to experience this life. The quality of your mind determines the quality of your life. Given this, it makes sense to examine its contents, understand it and train it! And that is what we will do together throughout the pages of this workbook with the use of guided journal prompts, research-based exercises, cognitive behavioural therapy worksheets, mindfulness practices and reflective writing. These tools will allow for slow and steady personal growth and self-development through increased self-awareness and self-exploration. This will, of course, require an investment from you and the commitment of your time, as and when you can give it. There are no prescribed timelines for this workbook and no expiry date. Each person will work their way through at their own pace and there is no right or wrong in this regard. Some of the work will be challenging but I encourage you to persist in spite of this because the insights gained and changes implemented will be *very much* worth it.

WHY WILL THE WORK BE CHALLENGING?

One of the reasons there are aspects of our characters that remain mostly, if not entirely, hidden from our day-to-day awareness is because we do not *want* to know about them. These are the parts of ourselves that we find too difficult or painful to integrate or that conflict with our morals and/or values, undermining our self-image. If this doesn't yet feel relatable to you, let me explain it from another perspective. I'm sure there are people in your life whose traits you can easily observe but to which they seem completely oblivious. Have you ever expressed a statement along the lines of the following?

- 'X is such a control freak'
- 'X is too needy'

- 'Why does X always go for the same type of partner over and over?'
- 'X is so cold'
- 'X is always bragging and showing off'
- 'Wow, X really gets defensive – they're such a hothead'
- 'X is such a drama queen'
- 'X thinks they're so perfect'
- 'Why is X always so uptight?'
- 'X is such a doormat'
- 'X always needs rescuing'
- 'Oh, X is always lying to themselves'
- 'X is so selfish'

These are insights into the obvious nature of a person's character via their repeated patterns of behaviour, yet they would most likely resent you for informing them of such insights.

Blaming the behaviour on a specific circumstance or some other external catalyst – 'I'm not usually like this, it's because …' or 'There might be some truth to that, *but …*' – is known as resistance, and I encourage you to observe your own resistance as you work through this journal. Keep a notebook nearby and make note of when it arises. If any section provokes a strong emotional reaction like irritation or the *insistence* that it simply does not apply to you, if you feel a block around picking up this journal to resume the work after a particular set of prompts, if you feel the urge to skip a section or zip through it, this is resistance and you need to ask yourself these questions:

- 'What is it I am feeling?'
- 'Where am I feeling it in my body?'
- 'What is this reminding me of?'
- 'Has this come up for me before?'
- 'Why is this my reaction?'

There is not *always* a deeper meaning to these reactions, but if you reflect with patience and honesty you will find that surprisingly often there is. These self-observations can be difficult but they are the roots of insight. There is real peace and clarity to be found on the other side of truly understanding yourself. It is a very worthy expenditure of your time and effort, so let's jump right in with something (possibly challenging or a little uncomfortable) for you to consider …

Has anyone ever told you something about yourself that deeply upset you or made you respond defensively? Looking back on the experience now, is there any element of truth in what the person said?

_____

_____

_____

_____

_____

MINDFULLY SELF-REFLECT AND BRING AWARENESS TO OUR EXPERIENCE

Now take a moment to bring your awareness to how you're feeling before we start this contemplative journey together. Jot down why you chose to pick up this journal, what your expectations are, what you hope to gain from giving your time to these practices and a broad sense of how you're feeling here at the outset.

_____

_____

_____

_____

_____

_____

_____

_____

_____

_____

_____

_____

_____

_____

_____

_____

chapter 1
early childhood experience and attachment theory

'The first five years have so much to do with
how the next eighty turn out'

— BILL GATES

Childhood is a universal rite of passage, so the information in this chapter is something I think everyone should
be informed about and take some time to consider in relation
to themselves and their own life experiences. If you have read
Jump you will know I had a difficult relationship with my dad
growing up and that that relationship left an undeniable mark
on my adult life. My mam battled for decades with recurring
bouts of life-threatening illness, and that experience too left an
evident imprint on who I would become. We are all a product of
our childhoods and understanding the unconscious conditioning,

habits, beliefs and biases we have taken with us from these formative years is vital for our self-awareness. Until my late twenties I had no idea my childhood hurts were still running my adult life to the degree that they were. This is not something we are taught and generally not something we have any awareness of – until maybe we end up in therapy because these hurts have overwhelmed our coping mechanisms and started to interfere with the quality of our lives. Reflecting on our childhood is an enormously important part of the inner work, so let me explain a little more about why and how we will do this.

Born with the privilege of having their fundamental needs for survival – food, water and shelter – met, a child's core needs are then to be warmly cared for, seen, heard and allowed to authentically express themselves. Children do not have the capacity to process their emotional experiences and they require an attuned and loving parent to appropriately guide them through big emotions, to model self-validation, emotional regulation and self-soothing. There's a large and growing body of research highlighting the importance of early life, right up to early adulthood, on cognitive, social and emotional development. The first seven years are of particular importance because during those years we are entirely egocentric – meaning we often struggle to grasp the point of view of another and to emotionally differentiate between ourselves and others too: we simply do not have the abstract mental capacity for these tasks yet – and so we internalise everything that happens in our environment as having happened *because* of us. For example, if there is tension in our home after our caregivers argue, we perceive this as 'I am responsible for this tension and I must fix it.' Children will employ various techniques from the fight, flight, freeze, faint and fawn biological toolkit to do this (see Chapter 3, 'Navigating Conflict').

THE GROUNDBREAKING ACE STUDY

As children we are sponges for our environment and our development is explosive and rapid. We learn complex cognitive skills like language, abstract thinking and theory of mind alongside the values, norms and expectations of our families, our societies and our cultures. Psychologists have long known that childhood is awash with big and lasting developmental milestones, and the ACE study, conducted in the mid-nineties, highlighted most compellingly just how pervasive and detrimental certain experiences in childhood can be.[1] ACE is an acronym for 'adverse childhood experiences', and these experiences are not just a socioeconomic problem. The original study included 17,500 adults from a population that was 70 per cent white, middle class and college educated. ACEs are, in fact, incredibly common.

ACEs, otherwise known as traumas, are not always major life events. I spent years avoiding the work I needed to do because of this misconception. Not feeling seen or heard can be traumatic. A sense of helplessness can be traumatic. Being told you can't or shouldn't experience certain emotions can be traumatic. Having a parent who focused on appearance or made you feel lovable predominantly for attainments or achievements can be traumatic. Having a parent who could not emotionally regulate or attune can be traumatic. Having your reality denied can be traumatic – to highlight this as clearly as possible, consider this example: as a child you sensed that your parent was sad; you asked them, 'Why are you sad?' and they replied with, 'I'm not sad, I'm fine' (for your own good and so as not to burden you). This simple exchange can be traumatic to a child because it teaches them that their internal perception of the world is wrong, that they cannot accurately read their environment or the emotions of others around them. It teaches them that their instincts are flawed. This tiny, forgettable interaction may be profoundly destabilising. Trauma responses are subjective but ubiquitous and found in relatively trivial events.

Adverse childhood experiences were found to affect the development of the immune system and the hormonal system as well as brain development. In all cases ACEs increased certain health risks in later life – like someone's predisposition towards developing depression – and in some cases they even caused changes at a genetic level, activating or inactivating certain gene expression. That means that external stimuli from our childhood can quite literally get under our skin, changing our physiology and our psychology, often for life, unless we acknowledge and address them.

So how does exposure to ACEs affect the brains and bodies of developing children? Most obviously, adverse brain changes often make people more likely to engage in high-risk behaviours – like addiction or self-harm – in an attempt to soothe psychological distress. But even if there is no increase in these high-risk behaviours, the body's stress-response system is changed as a result of that response activating again and again. This system, which I will cover in more detail in Chapter 5, 'Understanding and Handling Stress', then goes from being an adaptive life-saver to a source of toxic stress, damaging our health and wellbeing. Children are especially sensitive to this repeated stress activation because they are also navigating major developmental milestones.

The ACE study contained just 10 questions, which examined experiences of abuse, neglect and household dysfunction in childhood. Some questions covered acutely obvious adverse experiences or traumas, while others were quite surprising – for instance, did you often feel that no one in your family thought you were important or special? That your family didn't look out for each other, feel close to each other or support each other? Each question in the study required a simple yes/no answer. Every yes equalled a score of 1. On completion, an individual's total ACE score would fall between 0 and 10. It is a confronting questionnaire, but, as I've mentioned, ACEs turn out to be *incredibly common* – 67 per cent of the population of the United States (home of the original study) scored at least one ACE, while one in eight people scored four or more ACEs. To give the importance of this study some context, it was found that the higher the ACE score, the higher the vulnerability for undesirable outcomes in later life. The results did not point to a predetermined outcome, but rather to a possible correlated tendency or predisposition. Underlying predispositions still require the influence of environment to act as a trigger. As such, it is absolutely possible to navigate adulthood without adverse early experiences ever re-emerging as problematic. However, keeping the focus on mental health, it has been evidenced that depression is four and a half times more likely for someone with an ACE score of 4 rather than 1, while suicidality is *twelve times* more likely for the same score difference. It is my strong belief that a thorough understanding of the whole spectrum of 'who we are' is essential for self-empowerment. If we are aware of our possible predispositions, we can account for them with our lifestyle choices and by controlling for other environmental variables. It puts us back in the driver's seat of our life. Examining our early life experiences gives us invaluable knowledge around our own unique constitution, arming us with the ability to act accordingly for prevention and healing.

SO WHAT IF AN INDIVIDUAL HAS AN ACE SCORE OF 0?

Firstly, they are in the global minority and have been given a wonderful, deserved head start in life. However, it is not all plain sailing from here, thanks to an evolutionary phenomenon known as **epigenetics**. Epigenetics is the study of heritable changes in gene expression, or how our experiences and environment can alter the way our genes work, activating certain genes that were previously inactive or vice versa. Emerging evidence supports the idea that these changes can be passed through generations via our DNA. (Identifying this is, of course, very challenging given the insufficiency of human studies and the scientific challenges in conducting such studies.) Research suggests that if your great grandparent, grandparent, mother or father experienced trauma, the unresolved changes to their DNA structure can be passed down to their offspring and on and on until this lineage is addressed and healed.[2] This is brilliant for survival – whatever hurt them may not now hurt you, thanks to your inherited temperament and predispositions. Unfortunately, our environments also change drastically as generations pass and so their epigenetic changes for coping and survival are not always best applicable to your lifetime, often causing more harm than good. There is also a large and growing body of research focusing on *in utero* and perinatal trauma, meaning that any chemically or hormonally unsettling events experienced by the mother during pregnancy and/or any trauma undergone in birth may also be inherited by the child. Given this information, does an ACE score of 0 even exist? Unlikely.

AND WHAT IF AN INDIVIDUAL HAS AN ACE SCORE OF 10?

To quote Robert Sapolsky, professor of biology and neurology at Stanford University, 'Childhood adversity can scar everything from our DNA to our cultures, and effects can be lifelong, even multigenerational. However, more adverse consequences can be reversed than used to be thought. But the longer you wait to intervene, the harder it will be.' This journal is your beginner's guide to intervention, after which you may have insights prompting you to seek further intervention or make certain lifestyle changes. There is also another exception worth mentioning: the ACE study did not take into consideration the positive experiences in our early life that can buffer us from the effects of adverse experiences by building resilience. 'There are people with high ACE scores who do remarkably well,' says Jack Shonkoff, a paediatrician and director at the Center on the Developing Child at Harvard University. Close relationships are key – having a loving and attentive grandparent, an understanding and encouraging teacher or a trusted friend you can confide in in childhood may mitigate the long-term effects of a high ACE score in adulthood.

Time to

Take a moment to bring your awareness to how you're feeling after learning about childhood trauma and the impacts of our early experiences. Write freely and without judgement, reflecting honestly on the emotions, thoughts and sensations that arose for you. Have they since left your body and mind or are they still with you? Did you have an intense emotional reaction or experience any resistance? Pause, focus your attention inwards and jot down what you find there, even if it seems unrelated or irrelevant.

_____

_____

_____

_____

_____

_____

_____

_____

_____

_____

_____

_____

*The root of compassion
is compassion
for oneself*

— PEMA CHODRON

YOUR (LIFE-CHANGING) INTRODUCTION TO ATTACHMENT THEORY

'Unless you make the unconscious conscious, it will direct your life and you will call it fate'
— CARL JUNG

If you have never heard of or read about attachment theory, get ready to have your self-awareness socks blown off. Your attachment style is thought to be the single most important factor governing your ability to form stable, lasting intimate relationships in adulthood. It can be a key contributor to your ability to trust others, give and receive affection, communicate effectively, manage your emotions, set boundaries and develop a sense of self-esteem. Again, you can thank your early life experiences for this default setting in later life. I have had to work really hard to understand and begin to resolve my own attachment style. It has been one of the biggest challenges of my adulthood and I am still a work in progress, but this knowledge has been so helpful for me and I hope it is for you too.

So what is attachment? Attachment relationships are formed in our early childhood, primarily with our mother and/or father, or other close proximity caregivers, depending on the unique structure of our family unit. They serve as the secure base from which a child can explore and learn about their environment. Children's obvious and observable attachment behaviours with their caregivers later develop into their adult 'internal working model' for more abstract concepts like love, affection and trust. Given that intimacy is such an important theme in adulthood, understanding this profound relationship between our early attachment and the ways in which we form relationships as adults has been one of the great contributions of modern psychology. There are four observable attachment styles in infants. These categories were developed by Mary Ainsworth in the 1970s, building on the earlier pioneering attachment work of John Bowlby, with her Strange Situation experiment. You can watch this experiment in action on YouTube – it's fascinating! (In these descriptions of the four attachment styles I'm going to replace 'mother' with 'caregiver' to make them more universally applicable.)

○ Secure attachment

This is a healthy-functioning attachment. The infant will use the caregiver as a secure base to explore their new environment, become distressed in the caregiver's absence and actively seek touch, comfort and interaction on the caregiver's return. The infant is easily soothed after their distress and will soon return to their exploration.

○ Anxious-ambivalent attachment

This is an insecure attachment style. The infant is often distressed by the caregiver's absence and appears to seek contact and comfort from them on their return. However, the caregiver is not willing or able to soothe the infant's distress, which results in an apparent seeking and then resisting of proximity by the infant. The infant often appears angered by the interaction.

○ Avoidant-dismissive attachment

This is also an insecure attachment style. The infant is often *not* distressed by the caregiver's absence and does *not* actively seek contact or comfort from the caregiver on their return. The infant may instead ignore or avoid the caregiver.

○ Disorganised or fearful-avoidant attachment

This is also an insecure attachment style characterised by disorganised behaviour. For instance, the child is very distressed by the caregiver's absence yet avoids or ignores them on their return or perhaps seeks proximity to a stranger instead. In this attachment style, it often appears that the caregiver is a source of fright or fear rather than comfort and safety.

So our attachment styles are determined by our primary caregiver's:

- Sensitivity and responsiveness
- Emotional intelligence and attunement
- Parenting style – the four parenting styles are authoritative, authoritarian, permissive and uninvolved. The best outcomes are from authoritative parenting, which is disciplined but also sensitive and responsive. The rest have varying degrees of unfavourable outcomes

for attachment. We will delve into this more in Chapter 3, 'Navigating Conflict'.

- Disruptions to or interferences with the functioning of *all* attachment relationships in a child's environment and the caregiver's own unresolved mental state related to trauma, loss, abuse or their own attachment issues

HOW DOES ALL THIS APPLY TO YOU?

As I mentioned, our childhood attachment styles (however they are acquired) are predictive of how we'll develop – having enormous, unavoidable effects on our romantic relationships in adulthood.

○ Securely attached children become autonomous adults

These are adults who trust easily, desire long-term intimacy and value interdependent relationships. Interdependent relationships involve two individuals who are self-sufficient, love and respect themselves and choose to share their lives with someone else because the union is better than the sum of its parts. This type of relationship is characterised by healthy boundaries, room for uniqueness alongside a shared common ground, effective communication and appropriate responsiveness, self-awareness, tolerance and a shared evolution. Even among securely attached partners these utopian types of relationships are rare because human beings are inherently flawed and all relationships require work.

Autonomous adults are accurately attuned to the emotions felt within themselves and by others. They are cooperative, flexible and able to resolve conflicts effectively, communicating their upsets without fear of being invalidated or rejected. They trust that their needs will be understood and met by attuned others, and if not, they have the tools to assess and self-soothe appropriately. They have a secure sense of self in relation to others.

○ Anxiously attached children become enmeshed adults

Even as adults they can still think a lot about their dependency on their parent(s) and worry about pleasing them. They have sensitive, reactive nervous systems and often struggle to control their emotional expression. This can result in 'acting out' aggressive and/or passive-aggressive behaviours when they feel their needs are not being understood, heard or met. The 'other' determines their self-worth and as such they are overly invested in and preoccupied with relationships. They have an excessive need for intimacy, which can manifest as 'demanding', 'needy' or 'nagging' codependent behaviours in their relationships.

Codependent behaviours can be:

- Obsessive focus on your partner's behaviour, trying to control, change or fix them
- A lack of healthy boundaries, which means you'll tolerate poor behaviour
- Separation anxiety and a fear of abandonment

- Self-betrayal and neglect of your own needs in order to gain love, approval or validation from the other

These types of behaviours are common, once again, because human beings are inherently flawed.

○ Avoidant children become dismissive adults

They are compulsively self-reliant, avoid emotional closeness and remain distant in relationships. They have trouble expressing themselves emotionally and comforting others, instead often defaulting to coldly intellectualising or rationalising their behaviours, keeping emotions at bay. They are not accommodating, flexible or able to effectively resolve conflicts, as they prefer to withdraw or leave. This is as a result of downplaying the importance of or need for intimacy or interdependent relationships with others. It is also a protective measure against underlying (often unconscious or unacknowledged) feelings of fear, unsafety or vulnerability.

○ Disorganised children become unresolved adults

They often have a negative self-view and low self-esteem. They desire closeness and intimacy and are often prone to codependency in relationships, but at the same time they have high anxiety and apprehension in relationships, resulting from a deep fear of rejection. They expect to be hurt and do not trust others to understand or meet their needs. They are often deeply confused by this conflict and lack the strategies to resolve it and get their needs met.

Facts about anxious-avoidant partnerships

Anxiously attached adults and avoidant adults are frequently drawn to forming couples (this is an unconscious and quite magnetic phenomenon that may be an attempt at resolving the pathology via the other, which I'll explain in more depth in Chapter 9, 'Love and Relationships') and this combination is always especially fraught as a result of their opposing emotional quirks.

The dating pool is largely made up of avoidants. Speaking in very general terms, securely attached adults usually form healthy, long-lasting relationships and so are the least represented attachment style in the dating pool, as they are usually off the market. Anxiously attached adults find their self-worth in relationships and are often inclined towards codependent behaviours, so even if their relationships don't last, they will hop from one to the next – often repeating that anxious-avoidant union – rarely remaining single for long. Avoidant adults make up the majority of the dating pool, as they are very good at suppressing that evolutionary pair-bonding imperative, downplaying the importance of relationships and thus remaining single. Plus, avoidants rarely end up in relationships with other avoidants – which is self-explanatory: at least one person has to be interested in pursuing the relationship (past an initial burst of lust) for it to materialise! As such, the anxious-avoidant relationship is a very common phenomenon, with literally millions of couples playing out this tug-of war pairing around the planet right now.

If this extract resonates with you, you may be in an anxious-avoidant partnership:

An anxiously attached person in a relationship will have the characteristic feeling of not being properly appreciated and loved. They would – they tell themselves – like so much more closeness, tenderness, touch and sex – and are convinced that such a union could be possible. The person they are with, however, seems to them humiliatingly and hurtfully detached. They are hugely saddened by their coldness and distance, and gradually fall into moods of self-loathing and rejection, feeling unappreciated and misunderstood, as well as vengeful and resentful. For a long time, they may keep quiet about their frustrations until eventually desperation erupts. Even if it is a very inappropriate moment (perhaps they and their partner are exhausted and it is past midnight), they won't be able not to insist on addressing issues right now. Predictably, these sorts of fights go very wrong. The anxious lover loses their calm, they exaggerate and drive their points home with such viciousness that they can leave their partner convinced that they are mad and mean. A securely attached partner might know how to soothe the situation, but an avoidant one certainly doesn't. Tragically, this avoidant party triggers every insecurity known to their anxious lover. Under pressure to be warmer and more connected, the avoidant partner instinctively withdraws and feels overwhelmed and hounded. They go cold and disconnect from the situation, only further ramping up the partner's anxiety. Underneath their silence, the avoidant one resents feeling, as they put it, 'controlled'; they have the impression of being got at, unfairly persecuted and disturbed by the other's 'neediness'. They may quietly fantasise about going off to have sex with someone else completely, preferably a total stranger, or of going into the other room and reading a book, but probably not one about psychology.[3]

You can likely decipher your own attachment style by applying the information you've read so far to your own experience – but if you'd like further clarification, you can take an online questionnaire version of the Adult Attachment Interview, formulated by Mary Main in 1985. Make sure to take the test alone and answer the questions with absolute honesty, *as opposed to how you think you should*! This is invaluable knowledge to learn about yourself.

The online test covers 50 questions and should take you approximately 20 minutes to work through, with your attachment style calculated on completion. To find the test I recommend, search for 'Psychology Today Attachment Style Test'.

It is worth noting that humans are complicated, nuanced creatures, so it is difficult to place us neatly into rigid, entirely consistent categories. While we all have a *predominant* attachment style that will usually play out on repeat throughout our lives, it is also possible to shift attachment styles in context – meaning that we will often behave a certain way within certain environments or with certain people. Our predominant attachment style can also be influenced by particularly good or particularly bad romantic relationships that we experience in later life.

Again, if you've read *Jump* it will be clear from the narrative that I had a predominantly fearful-avoidant or disorganised attachment style for most of my early adulthood, confusingly swinging between avoidant and anxious behaviours in my relationships: coldly dismissing their importance while passive-aggressively seeking validation of the fact that I was absolutely loved and valued; leaving before I could be left but often not before continually betraying my own needs to appease my partner. The remedy, as ever, is simply knowledge. Being informed about attachment theory and the predictable patterns of behaviour it produces in all humans allows you to understand yourself, grasp where these aspects of yourself come from and communicate them to others. There is a huge difference between unconsciously acting out one's attachment style and holding oneself accountable for these impulses before, during or even after your antics have run their course. We cannot – most of us – have that utopian mutually secure, interdependent relationship I touched upon earlier (at least not without both parties committing entirely to a lot of personal and shared work over a lifetime), but we can have something almost equally wonderful: self-awareness.

If you found this topic particularly interesting, as many do, I highly recommend some further reading around it – most notably the book *Attached* by Amir Levine and Rachel S. F. Heller.

Time to

Take a moment to bring your awareness to how you're feeling after working through that exercise. Write freely and without judgement, reflecting honestly on the emotions, thoughts and sensations that arose for you. Have these emotions and thoughts since passed through your awareness and left? What about the sensations in your body? Did you have an intense emotional reaction or experience any resistance? Pause, focus your attention inwards and jot down what you find there, even if it seems unrelated or irrelevant.

_____

_____

_____

_____

_____

_____

_____

_____

_____

_____

_____

_____

_____

Time to

ENGAGE IN SOME REFLECTIVE LETTER WRITING

Our deepest and most painful emotional wounds, both conscious and unconscious, are held in the amygdala (the brain's fear centre) and the amygdala has no sense of time – meaning our deepest and most painful emotional wounds have the same effect on our emotional brain years and even decades later. This is why you may encounter someone who can speak about a traumatic event in a dissociated way but overreacts to seemingly small slights, which are triggering the unresolved implicit memory of the event that is stored in the subcortical emotional brain rather than the rational prefrontal cortex.

Letter writing (with a pen and paper, not a keyboard) is a very powerful tool – first, because it utilises the sensory motor cortex of our brain, which allows for the neurological integration of emotion, and second, because that subcortical emotional or subconscious brain cannot tell the difference between a written expression of emotion and a physical one occurring in the presence of the person you are writing to. Expressing that emotion in writing will have the same relieving effect on the unconscious brain and the brain's fear centre as would having that conversation in reality. It is a truly cathartic means of reflecting upon, accepting, integrating and releasing pent-up feelings.

Writing is the antidote to confusion. So if it feels right for you, you may also want to take the time to write a letter to one or both of your primary caregivers here. Is there something you need or want to say that you have never been able to? Has the work in this chapter triggered any unresolved emotions that you feel need to be expressed? As always, try to write in an unstructured, even ungrammatical, way and without judgement.

chapter 2
our core psychological challenges

'To be is to be vulnerable'
– NORMAN O. BROWN

Beyond the inescapable conditioning we all bring with us from childhood, every one of us will also have to navigate the universal core psychological challenges of simply being human. These are:

○ Bearing our need and dependency on others

As a species we have a particularly long and vulnerable child-hood where we rely almost entirely on our parents to keep us alive and safe. As we examined in the previous chapter, 'If our needs aren't met during infancy when we're utterly vulnerable and helpless, if our parents make us feel unsafe in the world from early on, it will shape our ability to trust and depend upon other people for the rest of our lives.'4 As adults we live in an entirely interdependent world, where one could reasonably argue that any sense of separateness might be the greatest illusion of all. A large portion of the global population also grows up bombarded with the messaging and influence of an individualistic culture, which creates a truly painful inner conflict. Regardless of this additional cultural pressure, the issue of bearing our own need for and dependency on others lies at the core of the human experience.

○ Managing intense emotions

Again, this is something we covered in the previous chapter: babies and young children cannot manage their big emotions; they cannot self-regulate or self-soothe. They must learn these skills modelled by a caregiver or their intense emotions will always feel scary, overwhelming and destabilising. As adults, they will not feel safe in their bodies and will not be able to feel, validate or process their inner emotional landscape. 'If we grow up with caretakers who let us down, who don't provide the emotional support we need, we will always have a hard time managing our own feelings.'5 Even for an emotionally intelligent adult, managing intense emotions remains a universal and lifelong psychological challenge.

○ Developing a sense of self-esteem

We are a 'pack' species. In an evolutionary sense, being exiled from our tribe or community meant certain death and as such we care deeply about our standing in relation to others. 'Each of us needs to feel that we matter and have a place in the world; we need a sense of internal worth and to feel that the other people in our lives value and respect us.'[6] Managing our self-esteem and self-validation in a healthy and sustainable manner in relation to others is a core human challenge.

Before I delve into these further and offer an exercise to iden- tify which one(s) pose the greatest difficulty for you, let me first clear up the difference between a psychological *challenge* and a psychological *need*.

CORE PSYCHOLOGICAL NEEDS

Our human psychological needs were first captured and summarised in a triangular hierarchy as a theory for human motivation by American psychologist Abraham Maslow in the 1940s. Our most basic needs make up the lower tiers of the triangle, and our needs become more complex as we work our way up. According to this theory, our more complex needs emerge as we come to sufficiently satisfy the previous needs.

This theory was pioneering but is now viewed as too rigid and linear – humans are complicated, nuanced creatures, too messy to fit neatly into categories this clear-cut, simple and defined. For instance, many people will sacrifice their financial security or their romantic relationships in pursuit of esteem. And many others manage to attain love, acceptance and belonging while in a difficult socioeconomic position that threatens their access to nutritious food or safe shelter.

What was captured here was some of the concrete physiological and psychological needs that we must attend to for quality of life. But it also stumbled upon our more abstract psychological *challenges* – the overlap is there to be seen in the higher tiers of the triangle – in terms of relationships and self-esteem. Maslow's early work on motivation provided the foundation for this knowledge to emerge through later research and is the origin of our understanding of human needs and challenges.

Maslow's Hierarchy of Needs

SELF-ACTUALISATION
Desire to become the most that one can be

ESTEEM
respect, self-esteem, recognition, freedom, fortitude

LOVE AND BELONGING
friendship, intimacy, family, sense of connection

SAFETY NEEDS
psychological safety, personal security, health, resources, employment, a home

PHYSIOLOGICAL NEEDS
air, water, food, shelter, sleep, clothing, reproduction

And this brings me to our exercise, based on the work of Dr Joseph Burgo, a psychoanalyst and clinical psychologist, which will uncover the core psychological challenge(s) that are likely to trouble you most. Learning to bear the dependent nature of our personal relationships, managing our emotional lives without defaulting to faulty learned coping mechanisms and battling for a sense of self-worth are at the heart of every human experience. These challenges are instilled in us by evolution and as such they shape our lives. If you struggle with need and dependency you might have trouble forming lasting and satisfying relationships, either as a result of not opening up to the closeness required for true intimacy or because the vulnerability of being so open triggers anxieties that make you act out. If you struggle with strong emotions you may often get overwhelmed and overreactive or shut down completely, becoming unable to feel your feelings, perhaps finding it more comfortable and familiar to flee the situation altogether. If you struggle with self-worth you may lack the confidence to assert yourself in many areas of your life and battle with negative self-talk or self-loathing.

*There are three things
extremely hard:
steel, a diamond,
and to know one's self*

— BENJAMIN FRANKLIN

IDENTIFYING YOUR CORE PSYCHOLOGICAL CHALLENGES

The following statements are divided into six groups. Read through all the statements a couple of times – take it slowly – and see which grouping intuitively speaks to you the most. Remind yourself that no one is watching, there is no judgement, no right or wrong, and you do not have to answer as you *think* you should. Try to release the notion of who you'd like to be and instead challenge yourself to assess your true nature with radical honesty. This may take some patience and a few attempts.

I experienced great resistance with this exercise when I attempted it first. I read through each statement, decided nothing resonated with me and picked up my phone for a while. I came back to it again, this time deciding everything resonated with me, got overwhelmed and left it for the night. Coming back to it for a third attempt the following morning, I highlighted all the statements I felt were true to me, but at that point I still wasn't satisfied, so I reassessed again the morning after that. Over time I came to slowly identify most with Groups 2, 4 and 6, with **Group 6** eventually emerging as my core psychological challenge.

Give yourself permission to take your time with this work. If this kind of self-awareness was easily accessible to us and we could fly through these exercises with clarity and ease, we would all be gurus with impressive emotional intelligence and unlikely to have picked up this journal in the first place. It is normal for prompts and exercises to feel confusing, irritating, overwhelming and a whole host of other triggering emotions and bodily sensations.

Group 1

- I don't trust other people to be there when I need them.
- I keep getting involved with the same clingy type.
- Feeling too needy and dependent is a weakness.
- I rarely overeat or drink too much and I have a good handle on my appetite.
- Sex doesn't matter as much to me as it does to other people.
- If you want something done right, you should do it yourself.

Group 2

- When a problem comes up, I often fantasise that someone will 'fix' it for me.
- I don't exactly binge but I wish I had more control over my eating.
- When I get romantically involved, it's all-consuming.
- Sometimes I feel way too needy.
- Now and then I end up having sex on a date even though I know it's a bad idea.
- Other people seem to matter more to me than I do to them.

Group 3

- Strong displays of emotion make me uneasy.
- I almost never cry, except once in a while during a sad movie.
- I rarely get angry and never lose my temper.
- I'm an extremely nice person.
- I often start on something new and quickly lose interest.
- I worry that something bad will happen if I'm not extremely careful.

Group 4

- I often overreact to situations and feel bad about it later.
- It's not unusual for me to feel emotionally overwhelmed.
- I wish I didn't have these mood swings.
- I often feel disorganised and out of control.
- I've lost my temper more times than I care to remember.
- I feel as if I'm sitting on a whole lot of intense feelings.

Group 5

- I probably spend too much time in front of the mirror.
- A big part of my budget is for new clothes and taking care of my appearance.
- Other people often wish they had my looks/success/ personality.

- In terms of relationships, it's hard to find anyone who meets my standards.
- At parties, I love to be in the spotlight.
- It's not unusual for me to feel impatient with or contemptuous of other people.

Group 6

- I often feel 'beneath' my friends and acquaintances.
- I tend to beat myself up over mistakes I make.
- I often feel envious of other people and the lives they lead.
- I worry that other people look down on me.
- I have a really hard time with criticism and get very defensive.
- I wish I were someone else.

Make sure you have completed the exercise and are clear on which group you relate to most before reading on, as the summaries below may unconsciously affect your ability to honestly self-reflect.

People who relate most to **Group 1** statements have a hard time acknowledging their need and depending upon others. They will develop defences geared towards denying dependency and persuading themselves they don't feel desire or need.

People who relate most to **Group 2** statements become overwhelmed by their needs and desires. They will develop defences geared towards mastering themselves by gaining control over what they need.

People who relate most to **Group 3** statements likely feel uncomfortable with intense emotions. They will develop defences geared towards avoiding situations that might give rise to strong feelings or towards reducing the impact of such feelings when they arise.

People who relate most to **Group 4** statements often feel overwhelmed by their feelings. They will develop defences aimed to get rid of those feelings in various ways or to find ways to hold on to one feeling over another.

People who relate most to **Group 5** statements struggle with feelings of shame and low self-esteem. They will develop defences meant to convince themselves and others that the exact opposite is true.

People who relate most to **Group 6** statements struggle with feelings of shame and low self-esteem. They have developed defences that have largely (but not entirely) failed them. Their task is to acquire new and more effective coping skills.

With this insight you now have an awareness of the core psychological challenge(s) that trouble you most and how they are likely to present in your life. Keep this knowledge at the forefront of your mind as you work your way through this workbook, trying to spot how often it is at the heart of or influencing other behaviours, feelings or tendencies you begin to become aware of. Armed with this self-awareness (and based on how great a trouble you perceive this challenge to be for you now or as you work through this workbook) you could also choose to investigate it further and equip yourself with better coping skills through cognitive behavioural or talk therapy. If that is not an option for you, I highly recommend picking up Dr Joseph Burgo's book *Why Do I Do That?*, which attempts to empower you to do your own therapeutic self-development around your psychological challenge(s) and associated defences.

It is worth bringing our awareness to these challenges and deciding to do the work around them because left unattended they will present over and over in burdensome ways as we attempt to make important decisions at different stages of adulthood, captured in Erik Erikson's famous psychosocial stages of development:

- Intimacy vs isolation in early adulthood – *will I share my life with someone or live alone?*

- Generativity vs stagnation in middle adulthood – *will I produce something of real value?*

- Integrity vs despair in late adulthood – *have I lived a full life?*

Time to

Take a moment to bring your awareness to how you're feeling after working through that exercise. Write freely and without judgement, reflecting honestly on the emotions, thoughts and sensations that arose for you. Have they since left your body and mind or are they still with you? Did you have an intense emotional reaction or experience any resistance? Have you been introduced to a new aspect of yourself? Was it a part of you that had been completely or partially outside of your conscious awareness until now? Pause, focus your attention inwards and jot down what you find there, even if it seems unrelated or irrelevant.

When I first started to do inner work, I would get a physical pain in my heart when I reflected on certain topics and it took me years to connect the two. I never believed a psychological event could evoke a physical sensation like that! But the mind–body union is an incredibly powerful one – use your growing awareness to examine this fact.

_____

_____

_____

_____

_____

chapter 3
navigating conflict

'Whenever there is tension, it requires attention'
— GABOR MATÉ

How uncomfortable are you with conflict? If you're like most people, including me, the answer is extremely. And if you found yourself relating most to **Group 3** or **Group 4** in the last chapter, the answer is undeniable. Conflict is an inevitable part of *all* relationships, an enduring feature of being human and part of a social species, yet most of us still handle conflict very, very badly, avoiding it at all costs or falling into defensive reactions – at which point no real communication is happening, only trauma arguing with trauma. Neither party comes out of an exchange like this feeling seen, heard or understood, nor is the conflict generally resolved in any meaningful way. And that is, perhaps, the biggest shame because anger and defensiveness are always a protection against feelings of vulnerability, and thus conflict is always a lesson, a flashing arrow pointing us towards the aspects of ourselves we still need to attend to. An inability to effectively navigate and resolve conflicts simply perpetuates these unresolved wounds and triggers, often damaging our closest relationships, sometimes in irreparable ways.

The spectrum of emotions associated with conflict, even the more severe ones such as rage, are actually natural and sometimes very healthy human emotions. Yet we are often overwhelmed when we meet them within ourselves or in another. David Dunning, an American social psychologist, says, 'The scope of people's ignorance is often invisible to them,' and this surely rings true for you if you've ever found yourself in a seemingly unresolvable conflict with someone. Their inability to grasp your perspective, despite your best attempts to communicate it, can be both baffling and maddening, their tone, posture, expressions of contempt or dismissiveness, their sharp or nasty language a source of pain akin to a physical blow. Perhaps you're capable of some or all of these behaviours yourself sometimes too? I know I was before I understood myself and my relationship with anger.

Conflict, hatred, rage and contempt are a fact of life, no matter how many self-help books promise that we can or should rid ourselves of their very existence – we can't and shouldn't. We can only hope to better recognise, validate, navigate and express them when they inevitably arise within or around us. Contempt, in particular, is something we will be discussing again in Chapter 9, 'Love and Relationships'.

In this chapter we are going to examine your relationship with conflict – drawing on the work of American marriage and family therapist Vienna Pharaon – and work our way slowly through the journal prompts to follow. Again, a reminder to practise patience and self-compassion here. Memories and emotions may spill from you and you should feel free to fill pages with whatever streams of thought and free associations arise for you. Do not judge what comes up or feel the need to make it make sense – just let it flow until you have no more to write. Equally, you may meet resistance or frustration here, finding no memories to draw on and nothing much to write. If this is the case, just start with bullet points, even one – and that could be simply naming the emotion, thought or bodily sensation that came up for you immediately after reading the prompt.

If you've read *Jump* you will know I spent many years feeling nothing while expending a whole lot of energy in the pursuit of numbing my unacceptable emotions, so 'numb' and 'nothing' are valid feelings to note here. We are often taught from a young age that anger and conflict are bad or unacceptable and thus many of us have rapid, well-oiled defences built against them and the emotions associated with them. Some of the most conflict-oriented people I know would be the first to tell you they hate conflict! I too fell into that bracket a number of years ago. So acknowledging the lack of feelings or emotions aroused by an exercise can give us clues to what we're not quite ready to face within ourselves.

PARENTING STYLES

The parenting styles described below are based on the seminal work of developmental psychologist Diane Baumrind in the 1960s, which was later expanded by Eleanor Maccoby and John A. Martin in the 1980s. Which is most similar to the parenting style you experienced growing up?

○ Authoritative

This parenting style is high on both responsiveness and warmth, and expectations and boundaries. A boundary is anything that marks a limit: this can be an environmental, physical or psychological limit, making a clear distinction between what is acceptable and what is not acceptable in terms of behaviours, personal dignity and/or emotional harm.

This parenting style is characterised by assertive and reciprocal parents who set clear standards while also being flexible and fair. They might use 'let's talk about it' type statements.

○ Authoritarian

This parenting style is low on responsiveness and warmth, but high on boundaries and expectations. It is characterised by autocratic parents who create a structured environment with clear rules and enforce power and punishment while keeping emotions at bay. They might use 'because I said so!' type statements.

○ Permissive

This parenting style is high on responsiveness and warmth, but low on boundaries and expectations. It is characterised by indulgent parents who avoid confrontation and set few rules; the environment is lenient and non-directive. They might use 'you're the boss' type statements.

○ Uninvolved

This parenting style is low on both responsiveness and warmth, and boundaries and expectations. It is characterised by mostly absent parents who may have competing priorities or little time, or who behave in a neglectful or uninterested manner. The explicit or implicit message is that you are on your own.

Journal prompts

TO EXAMINE YOUR RELATIONSHIP WITH CONFLICT

How your parents dealt/deal with conflict with each other was/is …

_____

_____

_____

_____

_____

_____

_____

How your parents dealt with conflict with you growing up
was ...

_____

_____

_____

_____

_____

_____

_____

_____

_____

_____

This was challenging for you because ...

_____

_____

_____

_____

_____

_____

_____

_____

_____

_____

_____

How you coped with it was ...

_____

_____

_____

_____

_____

_____

_____

_____

_____

_____

How that coping mechanism shows up in your close
relationships (current or prior) is ...

_____

_____

_____

_____

_____

_____

_____

_____

_____

_____

DEFENCE MECHANISMS

Every one of us uses psychological defences – they are not a bad thing. In fact, when not overly relied upon they can help us to navigate the world without getting overwhelmed by it. All defence mechanisms have two primary functions: to distort reality in some way and to protect us against feelings and/or thoughts that are too difficult for the conscious mind to cope with. However, there are some scenarios where it is useful to catch our defences at work, hindering us from facing the reality of the problem at hand, and conflict situations are one such scenario.

Our default defence mechanisms remain almost entirely outside of our conscious awareness – they make up part of the background blueprint of who we are – so you may need to take some time to feel into this one. Think through past experiences with conflict in light of the descriptions below and see if you can uncover which defences resonate with you most.

○ Repression

This is the pushing of unwanted, unpleasant, painful or unacceptable emotions, impulses or thoughts out of awareness. We repress **unconsciously** and suppress **consciously**. Regardless of the method, these hidden feelings and urges will continue to exert their influence on our behaviours and interpersonal dealings. Do you never get angry? Do you avoid conflict at all costs? You may be repressing or suppressing these natural and unavoidable human feelings and interactions.

○ Denial

This is the refusal to accept reality or a fact that conflicts with our wishes or beliefs. The word 'denial', which has its origins in Freud's psychodynamic approach, has now made its way into colloquial language. Most of us can easily recognise denial in another – it is most obviously observed in substance abuse, grief, troubled relationships and heartbreak.

○ Displacement

This is the redirection or discharge of anger or hostility onto a more appropriate or safe target – for instance, fury at your boss or colleague displaced onto your spouse or child when you get home.

○ Projection

Projection is taking our unwanted emotions or traits and attributing them to someone else. An example is a very angry person who claims that everyone else is provoking his or her anger. In projection it's not us, it's them. (Unlike displacement, here the individual is **disowning** rather than **discharging** the unacceptable part(s) of themselves.)

○ Reaction formation

This is turning an unacceptable feeling or impulse into its exact opposite. For instance, acting out overcompensating behaviours towards someone you actually dislike.

○ Splitting

Otherwise known as black and white thinking, this allows a person to tolerate difficult and overwhelming emotions by removing the complicated grey area of reality, seeing someone as either good or bad, idealised or devalued. There is no middle ground with this defence.

○ Idealisation

Often found working in tandem with splitting, this is attributing overly positive qualities, hopes or expectations to another, allowing us to cope with anxiety, ambiguity or ambivalence by viewing them as perfect or uncomplicated.

○ Control

This is attempting to manage the self, the other and/or the environment. Control can be overt or covert. An example of covert control of both the self and the other in conflict is passive-aggressive behaviour, like stand-offish or sarcastic communication or the silent treatment.

○ Rationalisation

Everybody uses rationalisation. We could also call it making excuses or wishful thinking, or simply lying to ourselves. It is devising reassuring and self-serving but incorrect explanations for our true motives, like, 'What a stressful day! I deserve this ice cream tonight – just a little bowl. A little break will actually help me stick to this diet.' With this defence, we tell ourselves an element of the truth but deny the larger truth of the matter to excuse our own behaviour and avoid bad feelings about ourselves.

∘ Intellectualisation

While rationalisation offers plausible explanations for specific facts, intellectualisation seeks to keep the entire spectrum of distressing emotions at bay. The person who intellectualises devotes so much attention to the thoughts passing through their head that they have no room to notice what's going on in their body – the home of feelings and emotion. Even if they do register some anger or sadness they will quickly shift attention away from bodily sensations and back into the emotion-free zone of thought. There are people who get so adept with this defence that they almost sever the mind–body connection entirely and can no longer feel or place emotion in the body.

Journal prompts

TO EXAMINE YOUR DEFENCE MECHANISMS

Which psychological defence mechanism do you rely on to handle difficult emotions in your relationship?

_____

_____

_____

_____

_____

_____

_____

_____

How you protected yourself (psychologically and physically) growing up was …

_____

_____

_____

_____

_____

_____

How you protect yourself in your current close relationships is …

_____

_____

_____

_____

_____

_____

_____

STRESS RESPONSES

We will discuss these responses in more detail in Chapter 5, 'Understanding and Handling Stress', but for now, based on the descriptions below, try to simply bring awareness to which response you think you might display in times of stress or distress, and consider how this response might affect your ability to effectively navigate conflict.

All of these reactions are natural, evolutionarily instilled human responses to stress, and in all but the last response – 'fawn' – the brain regresses to our most primal survival instincts, disconnecting from our more advanced cognitive capacities, like reasoning!

○ Fight

This response is to confront the real or perceived threat aggressively. It manifests in domineering behaviours, seeking power and control over the situation, to restore a feeling of safety.

○ Flight

This response is to run from the real or perceived source of danger. It manifests in fleeing behaviours, physically vacating the threatening environment, isolating or distracting oneself.

○ Freeze

This response is to find yourself frozen, unable to move or act against the threat. It manifests in shutdown behaviours, mentally vacating the environment or disassociating, spacing out or even feeling out of body.

○ Faint

This is an extreme stress-survival response to perceived inescapable threat – a common example is fainting following the sight of blood or a syringe. Of course, this is less applicable to conflict situations but if this response applies to you (via the aforementioned example or otherwise) it is good to be aware that this is how your body reacts to distress and danger in your environment.

○ Fawn

This response is to feign or pretend. It manifests in compliant behaviours, pleasing at all costs, to defuse the situation. Fawn responses require a little more cognitive functioning and self-regulation than the previous automatic reactions.

Journal prompts

TO EXAMINE OUR STRESS RESPONSE

Which biological stress response do you rely on to handle unpleasant or frightening experiences in your environment?

_____

_____

_____

_____

_____

_____

What do your defence mechanism(s) and stress response protect you from as an adult?

_____

_____

_____

_____

_____

_____

_____

_____

What about this feels familiar from your past?

_____

_____

_____

_____

_____

_____

_____

_____

Which of the following negative words or phrases resonate with you most when you think about conflict?

- Cycles of shame or feeling ashamed
- Game playing, manipulation or passive-aggressive behaviours
- Vying for control
- Withdrawal
- Blaming the other
- Agreeing to disagree

_____

_____

_____

_____

_____

_____

_____

_____

What or how do you usually feel after a conflict situation?

_____

_____

_____

_____

_____

_____
_____
_____

The story you tell yourself about yourself after conflict is …

_____
_____
_____
_____
_____
_____
_____
_____

The way you want to show up in conflict from now on is …

_____
_____
_____
_____
_____
_____
_____
_____

Ultimately happiness comes down to choosing between the discomfort of becoming aware of your mental afflictions and the discomfort of being ruled by them

— YONGEY MINGYUR RINPOCHE

SACRED VALUES

Here we enter into a domain of universal human irrationality known as 'sacred values'. While uncompromising self-awareness, access to our rational, reasoning brain and a certain amount of levelheadedness is necessary to navigate conflict, sacred values are the key to conflict resolution and lasting peace. These values define who we are. They are the intangible (sometimes incomprehensible) ideas and ideals that we all hold about what is correct, right and fair – and they loom large in all people, everywhere. Beyond solving the nuts-and-bolts issues of a conflict, we have to understand, respect and acknowledge the hurts we have caused to what the other holds sacred.

'Symbolic concessions of no apparent material benefit may be key in helping to solve seemingly intractable conflicts,' writes anthropologist Scott Atran, and this holds steady for everything from countries at war to partners at war in an everyday domestic argument.[7] To make the intangible more tangible, here are some extreme examples. Throughout history, humans have been willing to kill or be killed for their flag. In 1980s Ireland, republican political prisoners died protesting, among other things, having to wear regular prison garb. We have all witnessed many examples of the hatred, violence and corrosive division that occurs when a religious, political or moral stance is challenged. Our symbolic and sacred values are very, very important to us. We often confuse the literal and the metaphorical and because of that there are metaphors we have died, and will continue to die, for.

In recognising someone's sacred values you are recognising their humanity. They feel absolutely seen and heard, which is the ultimate conflict remedy. So it stands to reason that no material or instrumental solution will ever create the same kind of peace as a genuine apology. This will come to make much more sense as we work through Chapter 6, 'Core Personal Values'. But for now, here's a genuinely useful template on how to make proper amends – I know I needed to have this skill spelled out for me in black and white numerous times before I fully grasped it:

- **Apologise:** 'I'm sorry for _____.'
- **Take accountability:** 'That was selfish/inconsiderate/ dismissive/unkind of me.'
- **Empathise:** 'I imagine my actions made you feel ...'
- **Validate:** 'I understand why you thought/felt/reacted the way you did.'
- **Make a commitment:** 'I promise not to behave like that again. The next time I feel that way I will ...'
- **Keep your promise!** Even a genuine apology means nothing without the actions to prove it.

When it comes to conflict and conflict resolution, try to always bear in mind that the quality of your communication can almost always be measured by the response that you receive

– this logic, of course, flounders when you are dealing with any kind of emotional abuse like narcissistic abuse, contemptuous vitriol or gaslighting. No one is responsible for the unacceptable actions or reactions of another in an abusive exchange.

Time to

MINDFULLY SELF-REFLECT AND BRING AWARENESS TO OUR EXPERIENCE

Take a moment to bring your awareness to how you're feeling after working through the prompts in this chapter. Have you been introduced to a new aspect of yourself? Was it a part of you that had been completely or partially outside of your conscious awareness until now? Did you experience any resistance? Pause, focus your attention inwards and jot down what you find there, even if it seems unrelated or irrelevant.

_____

_____

_____

_____

_____

_____

_____

_____

_____

_____

_____

_____

_____

_____

_____

_____

_____

_____

_____

Time to

ENGAGE IN SOME REFLECTIVE LETTER WRITING

We are coming back to the powerful tool of letter writing, first introduced in Chapter 1. Unresolved conflicts, both big and small, can be deeply troubling, lingering within us long after the interaction has ended. If it feels right for you, you may want to take the time to write a letter to someone who has hurt or upset you. Is there something you need or want to say to that person that you have never been able to? Allow yourself to be seen and heard by fully expressing yourself on paper. Acknowledge the humanity in this person through accepting that they did their best with what they knew at that time. Give yourself the sincere apology, love or sense of value you may have needed from this person and offer them your forgiveness in return, if you feel ready to.

Now, a second letter of even greater importance. If it feels right for you, you may want to take the time to write a letter to someone who *you* have hurt or upset. This time acknowledge your own humanity through accepting that you did your best with what you knew at that time, fully express your sincere apology, your love and/or value for that person and ask them for their forgiveness in return, if you feel ready to.

_____

_____

_____

_____

_____

_____

_____

_____

_____

_____

_____

_____

_____

_____

_____

_____

_____

_____

_____

You can repeat this letter-writing exercise as often as you like in your own time as you work through each unresolved conflict that arises from your past. Most of us have more than one! It's important to attend to each one with a clear mind and an authentic desire to explore the remnants of that exchange within you. If it is not possible for us to resolve our conflicts with another, we have the ability to resolve them within ourselves by using tools like this.

chapter 4

managing intense emotions

'Between stimulus and response there is a space.
In that space is our power to choose our response.
In our response lies our growth and our freedom.'
– VIKTOR FRANKL (AUSCHWITZ SURVIVOR)

O ur emotional landscape is what makes life rich. It is what gives us our drive, our passions and purpose. So when we talk about managing emotions, it is only in terms of those distressing, overwhelming or incapacitating ones – of course we want to let our joyous, heart-centred states take up full residency in body and mind! What we're focusing on here is the emotions that get the better of us and make our lives undeniably worse. I hate to be reductionist – and I will offer exercises throughout this chapter to assist you in your emotional mastery – but *by far* the best tools to put the reins on our emotional brains are mindfulness practices, like yoga and meditation. If you've read *Jump* you will know that the discovery of both of these tools changed me and my life, and I practise and share them to this day. After almost three decades of being unconsciously run by my unpredictable, transitory and fluctuating emotional brain, it blew my mind to slowly learn that I, in fact, had free will and access to a stable sort of clarity even in the midst of the biggest emotional storms.

All feelings are okay once we've mastered how to allow ourselves to fully feel them so that we can then manage them or simply let them pass by. But prior to this mastery, it is generally our **reactions** provoked by our uncomfortable feelings that will cause us difficulty, and mindfulness practices mitigate these reactions more viscerally and effectively then any cognitive tool available to us, in my opinion. Mindfulness practices teach us how to anticipate and prepare for emotional experiences through bodily awareness and presence of mind, as well as how to calm ourselves in the moments those experiences arise. They afford us that space between stimulus and response that Frankl talked about, the time to create alternative thinking patterns and strategies, to lay down new pathways in the brain (I cannot recommend enthusiastically enough Frankl's bestseller *Man's Search for Meaning*). This is critical to changing our emotional habits and learning about our inner emotional lives. When we mindfully train our attention to hover in the present, we build the capacity to do it at will and as needed

– like in times of intense emotion. If you don't already, I urge you to make space in your day to train in these invaluable, life-altering tools. Take up a meditation and yoga practice if you can, one or the other if that's more manageable. I cannot overstate the difference between practising one of these tools for even ten minutes per day as opposed to not at all. If this is the only lifestyle change you implement from this entire book, that would be an *incredible* start.

If even ten minutes is too much to ask, let me offer an even simpler introduction to mindfulness practices (I will not let up here!). And this is something you should try on top of your yoga and/or meditation practice, if you have already established one. Mindfulness is simply the art of noticing or paying attention, and this is something we can speckle throughout our day, to our enormous benefit, by using micro-meditations and habit stacking – this is the work of James Clear in his international bestseller *Atomic Habits*. For instance, every day we brush our teeth – so let's habit stack brushing our teeth with a micro-meditation. All that means is that you try to be completely present for the entire act of brushing your teeth instead of doing so while lost in thought about what you'll wear or what you'll have for breakfast or how much you hate your boss or your day's to-do list or whatever else. You can habit stack micro-meditations onto multiple small daily rituals: brushing your teeth at the start and end of each day, having your morning coffee, passing a certain landmark on your commute, every time you open your preferred social media app – this is a great one because you will also very quickly realise how often you mindlessly repeat this action! Once your micro-meditations become as effortlessly a part of your day as the habits they are stacked upon, you can add one or two deep mindful breaths to the equation. Breathing deeply into the belly, followed by a long, slow, steady exhalation with a five-second pause at emptied lungs.

If this all sounds just too simple to reap big benefits, I beg you to take my word for it. The research is robust[8] and incorporating even the smallest of mindful acts into your day is incredibly valuable for everything from emotion and stress management to better cognitive functioning, increased grey matter in the brain and even slower ageing!

For me, the problem with cognitive tools implemented alone is that they are something we use after the moment we really needed them has passed – they are a means of examining our emotional reactions in hindsight. This can be a difficult practice to sustain because the results are often slow and hard earned through uncomfortable reflection. However, done repeatedly over time these exercises will afford us new understanding and personal insights, and that will amount to change. Now if you combine the cognitive exercises outlined in this chapter with a mindfulness practice or two, then you're on a rocket to high-level emotional intelligence – arguably the most useful skill one can possess for a good life. As we've already established in Chapter 2, 'Our Core Psychological Challenges', managing intense emotion is a universal test, omnipresent in matters of relationships and self-esteem, so the exercises in this chapter will apply equally to **Group 1** right through to **Group 6**.

EMOTIONAL GUIDANCE SCALE

During our formative years, many of us were not given the language we needed to express how we felt. So let's start by expanding the language available to us around our feelings at any given moment by taking a look at an emotional guidance scale – this one is adapted from Esther and Jerry Hicks's *Ask and It Is Given*:

1. Joy/appreciation/empowerment/freedom/love
2. Passion
3. Enthusiasm/eagerness/happiness
4. Positive expectation/belief
5. Optimism
6. Hopefulness
7. Contentment
8. Boredom
9. Pessimism
10. Frustration/irritation/impatience
11. Overwhelmed
12. Disappointment
13. Doubt
14. Worry
15. Blame

16. Discouragement
17. Anger
18. Revenge
19. Hatred/rage
20. Jealousy
21. Insecurity/guilt/unworthiness
22. Fear/grief/despair/powerlessness

One of the simplest ways we can start to get a handle on our emotions is by bringing our full awareness to how we are feeling and naming that feeling. Emotional guidance scales help us to do this and they are also useful for navigating our way to a better-feeling place. For example, let's say you find yourself at number 20 on the scale, engulfed by or acting out of feelings of jealousy. You cannot jump from 20 back to 1 – instead, you would choose a more accessible emotion along the scale to start to move yourself from this bad-feeling place to a better-feeling place. This is how it works:

- Consulting your emotional guidance scale, choose a lower numbered emotion that is accessible to you and brings relief. (Don't try to jump more than two or three numbers up the scale at once, and only move one number at a time if that is what feels most authentic.)

- Settle into this new emotion; give it a 'felt-sense' in the body – feel into and acknowledge the physical sensation it gives you.

Repeat these steps slowly and until you find yourself embodying a much better-feeling emotion than where you started. Over time and with practice, recognising our feeling tone, investigating what underlies it and moving up the scale will become familiar and natural.

RAIN

To begin the work of investigating what underlies our difficult emotions, I'd like to introduce the powerful work of a hero of mine, PhD psychologist and advocate of Buddhist meditation Tara Brach. To deal with difficult emotion she proposes a practice of radical compassion with the easy to recall acronym RAIN:

Recognise what is going on.
Allow the experience to be there, just as it is.
Investigate with interest and care.
Nurture with self-compassion.

○ Recognise what is going on

This is consciously acknowledging, in any given moment, the thoughts, feelings and behaviours that are affecting you. This can be a done with a simple mental whisper, noting what you are most aware of. You can come back to the emotional guidance scale for this step if you have any difficulty naming the feeling you're experiencing.

○ Allow the experience to be there, just as it is

This is letting the thoughts, emotions, feelings or sensations you have recognised simply be there, without trying to fix or avoid anything. For instance, you might recognise fear and allow it by mentally whispering 'it's okay' or 'this belongs' or 'yes'. Allowing creates a pause that makes it possible to deepen our attention, as opposed to our reflexive reaction, which is to avoid, rid ourselves of or change unpleasant feelings or sensations.

○ Investigate with interest and care

This is calling on your natural curiosity – the desire to know the full truth behind your uncomfortable emotions. You might ask yourself:

- 'What is it that most wants attention?'

- 'How am I experiencing this in my body?' Simply name the bodily sensations you are feeling when the emotion arises (even if they appear unrelated at first) – for example, headache, dry eyes, tension in the jaw/shoulders, lump in the throat, quickening of the breath or tightness in the chest, any muscular contractions, any aches or pains and any digestive complaints.

- 'What is the story I am telling myself around this?' Listen closely to the inner narrative that accompanies the emotion. This will take a quietening and a focusing of your attention for a few moments. Tune into the automatic mental chatter. It might sound like 'he always does this' or 'she just doesn't care'.

Whatever the inquiry, your investigation will be most transformational if you step away from mental concepts and bring your primary attention to the felt-sense in the body.

∘ Nurture with self-compassion

Self-compassion should begin to naturally arise when you recognise that you are suffering. However, for many of us, this can often be the hardest part. To move into self-compassion, try to sense what the wounded, frightened or hurting place inside you needs most. Ask 'What does this vulnerable place most need from me?'

Then offer some gesture of active care that might address this need. Does it need a message of reassurance? Of forgiveness? Of companionship? Of love? Experiment and see which intentional gesture of kindness most helps to comfort, soften or ease your emotional discomfort. It might be the mental whisper 'I'm here with you', 'I'm sorry, and I love you', 'I love you, and I'm listening', 'It's not your fault. You are good.'

In addition to a whispered message of care, many people find healing by gently placing a hand on their heart or cheek, or by envisioning being bathed in or embraced by warm, radiant light. If it feels difficult to offer yourself love, bring to mind someone or something you love and have an **uncomplicated** relationship with – a spiritual figure, family member, friend or pet – and imagine their love flowing to you.

At this point, if it's still necessary, you can come back to your emotional guidance scale and take the steps we covered earlier to actively move yourself to a better-feeling place.

If you enjoy this more holistic, spiritual or mind–body approach to emotional management, there will be much more for you to engage with in Chapter 8, 'The Science of Awe and Gratitude'. If you are new to this work and you struggle to engage the mind–body connection – that is, if much of the above enquiry sounded alien or a bit weird to you – please don't worry. Just keep reading.

CBT TECHNIQUES

> 'If your emotional abilities aren't in hand, if you don't
> have self-awareness, if you are not able to manage
> your distressing emotions ... then no matter how
> smart you are, you are not going to get very far.'
> – DANIEL GOLEMAN

I was very mind–body disconnected when I succumbed to burnout, and for a long time afterwards. It took me quite a bit of patience and practice to regain that skill and you will too. But a more accessible entry point for you to begin to engage in investigative self-enquiry and managing difficult emotions may be practical cognitive behavioural therapy (CBT) techniques. I learned how to master and apply these tools through the work and mentorship of neuroscience lecturer and PhD researcher Brian Pennie. These are brilliant to come back to on occasion, even when you have a steady and habitual sense of mindful awareness. You will know when you need to, as you will use that awareness to recognise that your emotions feel unsettled, unfamiliar or distressing, your reactions are disproportionate or you're coping by suppressing or avoiding your feelings, which is always an unsuccessful and short-term tactic.

I'd like to offer three useful tools for you to trial and see which works best for you.

○ Cognitive reappraisal

This is based on the work of Richard Lazarus and his cognitive mediational theory of emotion. The human mind has the tendency to create an automatic assessment of any given situation. These assessments are done rapidly and often subconsciously. They are subjective in that each person understands what a specific situation means to them. To help manage the automatic assessments of the emotional brain in a stressful or overwhelming situation, we can use a reappraisal (or reinterpretation) strategy. For example, in an argument with a friend, we might re-evaluate the situation from their point of view, thereby stepping outside of our own emotional arousal and decreasing our emotional burden.

A practical tool for reappraisal is Socratic thinking, used to assess a stressful event, in the moment or afterwards, by examining your thoughts about that event, with the steps outlined below:

1. Detail the thought to be questioned.
   I am feeling panicked and fearful that my boyfriend is cheating on me on his night out – he hasn't replied to my text in over two hours.

2. What is the evidence for the thought? And against it?
   My ex, who cheated on me, was so unreliable with answering calls and replying to texts, he always left me feeling uncertain, unsafe and uncared for. I feel that this kind of behaviour indicates a lack of interest and respect. However, my new boyfriend has never otherwise let me down; he has given me no reason, prior to this, to think he would ever cheat on me. He has always made me feel safe, certain and valued.

3. Am I basing this thought on facts? Or on feelings?
   Although the fact is that my ex cheated on me, I think the current circumstance is based only on my feelings. Not replying to texts is one of many poor behaviours my ex displayed, so it is not a fact that not replying to my text automatically means my new boyfriend will cheat too.

4. Is this thought black and white, when reality is always more complicated?
   Yes, I am jumping to conclusions. There are many reasons why he may not have texted me back yet. I never feel this kind of intense emotion when his

replies are delayed while he is at work. I must be feeling vulnerable because he is on a night out.

5. Could I be misinterpreting the evidence? Am I making any assumptions?
   Yes, I think I am being triggered in the present by a hurt from the past. I am hypervigilant of ever having to feel the shame, humiliation and rejection of being cheated on again and so I am quick to spot that possible threat in my environment. I will not spiral into this negative assumption without any evidence – instead I will assume the best and communicate my needs clearly to my boyfriend in future.

Write your thought responses to each question and then elaborate, explaining 'why' or 'why not' when appropriate in your answers.

1. Detail the thought to be questioned.

_____

_____

_____

_____

2. What is the evidence for the thought? And against it?

_____

_____

_____

_____

_____

3. Am I basing this thought on facts? Or on feelings?

_____

_____

_____

_____

_____

4. Is this thought black and white, when reality is always more complicated?

_____

_____

_____

_____

5. Could I be misinterpreting the evidence? Am I making any assumptions?

_____

_____

_____

_____

I have many default reappraisal strategies that spring to mind as I navigate the ups and downs of my day-to-day, but my favourite one of all is **'this is not personal'**. Once you start to study the human mind, you learn quickly that very little anyone says or does is because of you, yet for some reason we love to take things personally – causing ourselves so much unnecessary turmoil. A person's behaviour is a projection of their own reality and a reflection of how they feel about themselves. Life gets so much easier when you accept this simple fact.

○ The ABC technique

This CBT tool for managing intense emotion is based on the work of psychologist and researcher Dr Albert Ellis. This technique assumes that our beliefs about an event affect how we react to that event. If we have inaccurate beliefs about a situation, our response may not be effective or healthy. The ABC model helps with emotional functioning by recognising how our thoughts influence our feelings, physical sensations and behaviours, identifying the inaccurate beliefs underlying our thoughts and creating space to consider whether they're true, which counteracts needless distress and improves how we choose to react.

This is what the ABC technique looks at:

A: Adversity or activating event.
B: Your beliefs about the event, both rational and irrational, including both obvious and underlying thoughts about situations, yourself, and others.

C: Consequences, which includes your behavioural or emotional response.

So B is the link between the event and our reaction. If we can examine, challenge or change our beliefs, then it stands to reason that we can create more positive outcomes. Using the ABC technique, you focus on your behavioural or emotional responses and try to peel back the automatic beliefs that might be behind them. Once uncovered, you can then examine or re-evaluate these beliefs.

Here are examples of some benign events that our underlying automatic beliefs could turn into an irrational thought spiral, leading to an array of negative emotions ranging from anger, sadness or anxiety to guilt, fear or even shame:

- Your colleague arrives at work but doesn't greet you.
- You're friendly with all your classmates, but one of them hosts a party and doesn't invite you.
- Your cousin is planning her wedding and asks your sibling, instead of you, to help.
- Your friend doesn't follow up with lunch plans.
- Your partner is in a bad mood.
- Someone unfollows you or doesn't engage with you on social media.

Working through the ABC technique looks like:

A: Describe the activating event.
Susan arrived into work today and didn't say hello to me.

B: Detail your rational thoughts about the event.
I thought she must be in a bad mood and perhaps something had happened in her personal life or on her way into the office.
Detail your irrational thoughts about the event.
I thought I must have upset her at the meeting yesterday – maybe she was off with me afterwards and I didn't notice. I'm not sure she likes me, even on a good day, and I think I have annoyed her and now she's stopped even pretending to like me. I feel rejected, ashamed and embarrassed. There's no way I can talk to anyone about this. The office is going to be so awkward. I feel so uncomfortable. She'll definitely gossip about me with Lucy and Hannah.

C: What were the consequences of your irrational thoughts?
My mood was noticeably changed. I did not feel good and even noticed my hands were sweaty. I felt jittery and on edge. It really ruined my morning. I couldn't concentrate on my work well into the afternoon. I was out of sorts and short with another of my colleagues because of it. I avoided Susan, Lucy and Hannah all day. I just wanted to get home and away from that environment.

A: Describe the activating event:

_____

B: Detail your rational thoughts about the event:

_____

_____

_____

_____

_____

_____

Detail your irrational thoughts about the event:

_____

_____

_____

_____

_____

_____

C: What were the consequences of your irrational thoughts?

_____

_____

_____

_____

_____

_____

Over time, you'll learn how to recognise your underlying beliefs (**B**) about certain events (**A**) and this will allow space and opportunity for healthier consequences (**C**) and more positive emotions.

Irrational Beliefs

Probably the number one irrational human belief is 'everybody has to like me'. If we sense (or tell ourselves) that someone doesn't like us, it taps into our unconscious but powerful abandonment schema and makes us feel fundamentally unsafe – something all humans hate. But, of course, not everyone is going to like us, so this irrational belief just creates cycles of unnecessary suffering. Plus, someone not liking us is okay once we definitely like ourselves.

○ Cognitive restructuring

Our last CBT tool for managing intense emotion, based again on the work of Dr Albert Ellis, is cognitive restructuring. Again, this technique works on the grounds that how we habitually think influences how we habitually feel. Or, said another way, how we feel is not the result of what happens to us: it's the result of how we **think** about what happens to us. Cognitive restructuring forces us to slow down, become more aware, reflect instead of react, break bad mental habits, think more clearly and rationally, and gain a sense of agency and control in situations of emotional hijacking – something we *all* experience.

Cognitive restructuring is done using a six-step thought record, as follows.

    ° STEP 1: Pause

Use a feeling of strong negative emotion as a **cue to pause** instead of acting on instinct:

- Feel anger = lash out
- Feel anxious = hide
- Feel sad = have a beer

I felt a burst of pure rage after being unfairly cut off when I had the right of way.

This step teaches us to inhibit our instinctual response to negative feelings and instead approach them with a sense of curiosity.

- Feel anger = your cue to pause
- Feel anxious = your cue to pause
- Feel sad = your cue to pause

    ° STEP 2: Identify the trigger

Triggers are often external but more times than we probably care to admit the source is internal: the origin of our distress is our own thoughts. To identify the trigger for our negative emotion we ask ourselves four questions:

- Who was present with me at the time I got upset/angry/anxious?

  My partner was travelling with me in the car.

- What happened?

  I was feeling tired and a bit irritable after a long week at work. My partner had taken longer than expected to be ready to leave the house so we were also running late for our restaurant booking. While en route, I was dangerously cut off by another car when I had the right of way.

- When did I first start feeling upset/angry/anxious?

  When I think about it, I was probably wound up all day. I woke up this morning feeling like I'd got out of the wrong side of the bed, my work day was a slog and I just wanted to get to the restaurant to decompress a little. I was pretty irritated at my partner for causing us to be late and putting me under more pressure. I was already feeling angry pulling out of the driveway.

- Where did it all occur?

  The burst of rage occurred in the car. I couldn't help it – I was shouting and cursing. I drove erratically after the car that had cut me off and beeped at them several times. I followed the car closely until it turned off in the opposite direction, but the feeling of rage stayed with me for quite some time. I didn't enjoy our meal and my partner was very off with me after the outburst.

∘ STEP 3: Notice your automatic thoughts

As we've already established, these are our default, immediate interpretations of an event. They come in the form of self-talk, mental images and memories. Most of the time we don't notice our automatic thoughts or we're only vaguely aware of them. This step asks us to build the habit of bringing our full awareness to these thoughts during experiences of strong negative emotion.

My initial reaction was a feeling of pure hatred towards whoever was driving that car. They were barely human to me – I wanted to scream every awful thought I was having at them. When I removed my hand from the horn I thought, 'This kind of stuff always happens to me, I'm so unlucky.' I then started to imagine all the things my partner must have been silently saying about me. That made me feel annoyed and defensive and I started to formulate all the reasons my rage was completely justifiable.

∘ STEP 4: Identify your emotional reaction and note
how intense it was on a scale of 1–10

This step is self-explanatory. If you find it difficult to name your emotions, revert to the emotional guidance scale for assistance.

I was incredibly angry and filled with rage – I would say it was at least a 9.

∘ STEP 5: Generate alternative thoughts

Similar to our reappraisal strategy, this technique asks you to step back from automatic assumptions and allow space for alternatives.

I think I was discharging my pent-up, unexpressed frustrations from the entire week in this one incident. It was a hugely disproportionate reaction. Imagine if I had actually caught with up that car, if I had had the chance to scream all the things I was thinking at the driver, only to discover it was a young mother rushing her sick child to the hospital? It might have been an elderly person who was nervous on the roads or someone from another country unfamiliar with the rules, or even just someone absorbed in their own troubles after their own tough week.

∘ STEP 6: Re-rate your strong negative emotion now
after generating alternative thoughts

When I see how wound up I already was and when I stop thinking about it as a personal attack done on purpose, I could rate my emotions at about a 2, and I feel a little ashamed and embarrassed.

THOUGHT RECORD

STEP 1: Pause
Okay, what happened here?

_____

_____

_____

_____

_____

STEP 2: Identify the trigger
Who, what, when, where, why?

_____

_____

_____

_____

STEP 3: Notice your automatic thoughts
What thoughts were running through my mind immediately after the trigger?

_____

_____

_____

_____

STEP 4: Identify your emotional reaction and note how intense it was on a scale of 1–10
What emotions am I feeling right now? How intense are they?

_____

_____

_____

_____

_____

STEP 5: Generate alternative thoughts
What are some alternative – ideally more realistic – ways of interpreting what happened?

_____

_____

_____

_____

STEP 6: Re-rate your emotions
How intense are my emotions right now?

_____

_____

_____

_____

_____

While there is some clear overlap in these tools, they approach from slightly different angles, and this is important in finding the one that will work for you. Does it resonate with you most to ask 'why' in pursuit of reappraisal? Do you think you may benefit more from challenging your negative beliefs or thought spirals? Or do you want to learn to use intense emotion as a cue to pause, step back and reassess?

This is work every single one of us can benefit from, whether or not we perceive our emotional reactions to be problematic. Research shows that repetition of new skills, until they become part of your daily routine, is the main factor in learning new behaviours, so when you decide on the approach that works best for you make sure to implement it daily for at least 30 days to see real change. Be patient with yourself and focus on learning or unlearning one behaviour at a time. We will come back to this strategy for implementing change in Chapter 10, 'Future-Self Journalling'.

If you found these CBT worksheets useful and would like to continue to investigate this work, I highly recommend the *Relaxation and Stress Reduction Workbook* by Martha Davis, Elizabeth Robbins Eshelman and Matthew McKay where you will find some brilliant practical resources for dealing with and overcoming strong and destabilising emotions like fear, anger, worry and anxiety. And of course there's always the option of doing an 8- to 12-week course of CBT with a trained therapist.

By understanding our emotions, we can understand how

we react to stress, and that brings me nicely to our next chapter, 'Understanding and Handling Stress'.

Time to

MINDFULLY SELF-REFLECT AND BRING AWARENESS TO OUR EXPERIENCE

Before moving on, you may want to take a moment to bring your awareness to how you're feeling after working through that chapter, always paying attention to any resistance. Pause, take a deep grounding breath and focus your attention inwards. Use the self-awareness we have been developing at the end of each chapter before this one and jot down whatever comes to mind.

_____

_____

_____

_____

_____

_____

_____

_____

_____

_____

_____

_____

_____

understanding and handling stress

'Rule number one is, don't sweat the small stuff.
Rule number two is, it's all small stuff.'
— ROBERT S. ELIOT

Now, if only our wonderfully instinctual and reflexive stress response system could come to terms with those rules above. Despite our best efforts to live by those sentiments, stress is unfortunately another inescapable fact of life. And though it is vilified, not all stress is bad – in fact, without it things would be a little boring. So, let's first set about understanding stress and how it affects our minds, bodies and behaviours.

Having suffered from a fairly catastrophic (yet strangely unforeseen) burnout in 2017 – depicted to the best of my (slightly traumatised) ability in the pages of *Jump* – I am enormously enthusiastic about explaining the role of our body's stress response system and how we can learn to modulate it to avoid anxiety, burnout and illness. I am also lucky enough to have learned from some of the leading figures in this field of research. This chapter was written in collaboration with Ray McKiernan, director of Resilience International and the Stress Management Institute of Ireland. If you find the ideas in this chapter useful, you can access much more information on the websites www.resilienceinternational.com and www.stressmanagement.ie.

UNDERSTANDING STRESS

Stress is the tension created in our bodies by the fight or flight response, an automatic survival system we all share and the manifestations of which – fight, flight, freeze, faint, fawn – we touched on in Chapter 3, 'Navigating Conflict'. It developed in our prehistoric ancestors to generate a quick mobilisation of energy in reaction to perceived threats in our environment. During this stress response dozens of physical changes occur to support exertion, including an increase in blood pressure, heart rate and muscular tension. Simultaneously, other systems divert energy to these survival functions, resulting in a decrease in the workings of the digestive, reproductive and immune systems. Our body sees it like this: we won't have much use for those long-term operations if we're dead.

Unfortunately, these days that same ancient reflex is stimulated far too often – not only by stressors in our environment, but also by stressors in our bodies and minds. These troubles and worries demand our attention and drain our energy throughout the day.

Here are some common daily stressors we all encounter:

◦ Environmental stressors

Tangible stressors in our environment are things like too much heat or cold, noise, traffic jams, pollution and bad weather. Interpersonal stressors are things like miscommunications, disagreements and differences in personalities, goals, values or communication style, or on the flip side, restrictions to our social engagement. Work stressors might include things like poor communications, poorly delivered performance feedback, distractions, interruptions, deadlines, malfunctioning equipment, poor teamwork, role ambiguity, someone using your labelled milk and so on.

◦ Bodily stressors

These include serious illness, tiredness, aches and pains, jittery nerves from low blood sugar, digestive discomfort, muscle fatigue, headaches and so on.

◦ Mental stressors

These include grief, loss, heartbreak, negative self-talk and self-doubt (something we'll address in Chapter 7, 'Self-Limiting

Beliefs and Negative Self-Talk'), anxiety, worry, obsessive thinking or rumination, taking things too personally, suppressing or avoiding our feelings.

These categories of stressor all overlap and influence each other constantly. To demonstrate, consider this series of events.

You have a meeting at 7.30 a.m. on Monday (**environmental stressor**). You wake at 6 a.m. to the shrill sound of the alarm clock (**environmental stressor**) and immediately feel tired (**physical stressor**) and resentful (**mental stressor**) that you have to get up so early. You make your way down the dimly lit hallway and trip over someone else's shoes (**environmental stressor**). You feel an ache in your toe (**physical stressor**) as you limp into the bathroom only to become more irritable (**mental stressor**) when you find someone has already used all the hot water (**environmental stressor**). You make it out of the house and into the car where the gauge on the dashboard tells you that you're almost out of petrol (**environmental stressor**). You worry (**mental stressor**) that you may not have enough to make it to work on time for the meeting (**environmental stressor**). You drive onto the main street and into a traffic jam due to roadworks (**environmental stressor**). You grind your teeth (**physical stressor**) at the poor city planning and resent out loud (**mental stressor**) what they're doing with all your tax money (**environmental stressor**). Arriving to work with a headache (**physical stressor**), you walk into the meeting five minutes late to hear someone sarcastically say, 'Nice of you to join us' (**environmental stressor**). You bite your tongue (**physical stressor**) and feel distracted by your accumulated frustrations (**mental stressor**) for most of the meeting. And your day has just begun …

Our bodies react to all our modern daily hassles the same way they did to being chased by a tiger thousands of years ago, and this leads to an accumulation of tension which can strain certain bodily systems and lead to illness. But as I mentioned, not all stress is bad news – in brief bouts it can be helpful in improving our concentration and endurance. It allows us to speed up for a little while and increase our productivity. However, we need to be able to pace ourselves and balance our tensions. This is the basic premise of managing stress. By learning to better manage our efforts when possible, we can prevent unnecessary wear and tear on the systems of our body.

THE HUMAN PERFORMANCE CURVE

The **Human Performance Curve**, based on the the work of psychologists Robert M. Yerkes and Dillingham Dodson in 1908, provides a visual display of our optimal range for performance and wellbeing.

The graph on the next page highlights the three possible pressure scenarios we face.

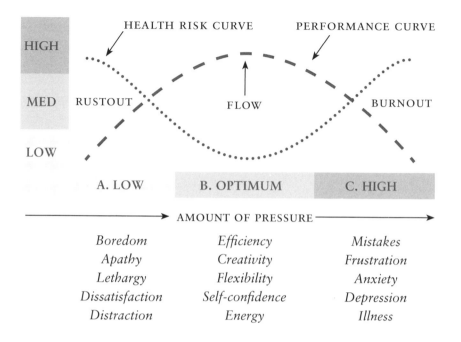

	HEALTH RISK CURVE	PERFORMANCE CURVE	
HIGH			
MED	RUSTOUT	FLOW	BURNOUT
LOW			

A. LOW	B. OPTIMUM	C. HIGH

AMOUNT OF PRESSURE

Boredom	*Efficiency*	*Mistakes*
Apathy	*Creativity*	*Frustration*
Lethargy	*Flexibility*	*Anxiety*
Dissatisfaction	*Self-confidence*	*Depression*
Distraction	*Energy*	*Illness*

A. Too little pressure: here we find low performance yet high health risk – our wellbeing actually suffers when we have too little to challenge us. Stress is not all bad.

B. Optimum pressure: here performance is at its highest and health risk is at its lowest. We are in eustress (or good stress), which some call *flow*.

C. Too much pressure: here we see diminishing performance alongside a dramatic increase in risk to health and wellbeing. Too much stress for too long is very bad.

To make this *extra* clear (did I mention I'm passionate about this topic?), an unhealthy stress reaction in the body looks a little like a stairway to burnout – a steady rise into that high-pressure zone with barely a glance back before we plummet into the quicksand of disengagement and distress.

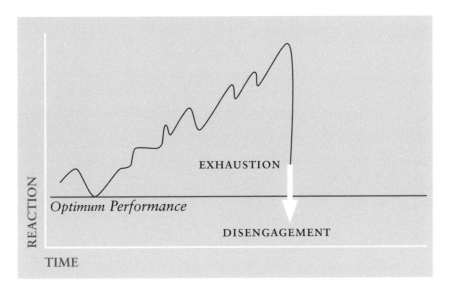

This climb happens slowly over time. How much time? Well, that depends on each individual's access to external and internal resources and their ability to temporarily cope with the mounting pressures of life. For me, this climb to collapse took approximately 12 to 18 months, with the last 3 months noticeably accelerated, and that's speaking in hindsight! By that point I was so wound up I had lost touch with reason and insight. High levels of stress impair the higher functioning and abstract thinking necessary to modulate, introspect, delay gratification and anything else that may have helped me. I really didn't have the wherewithal to see what was happening to me or have any idea how to slow or rectify it. I just wavered back and forth on that perilous cliff edge for about 12 weeks until the last of my resources and coping skills were exhausted. If you're interested to know what life is like when you freefall off the edge, that grey listless reality is also described in the pages of *Jump*.

I now know that a healthy bodily reaction to stress is not without those periods of high pressure. I repeat: we need stress! The difference is that our response to that stress is modulated through learned insight, self-awareness, interoception (the understanding of our bodies' inner sensations), deliberate action and acts of self-care, which allow for periods of down-regulation. A healthy response looks like this:

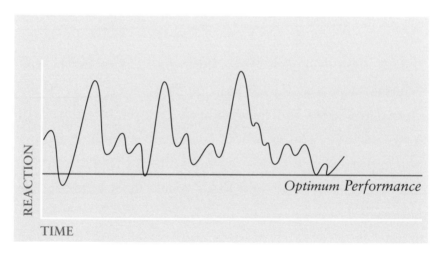

REACTION

Optimum Performance

TIME

To make sure our bodies balance like this in response to environmental, physical and mental stress, we have to learn the tools to pace ourselves, maintain our wellbeing and stay in that optimum pressure zone by building bodily awareness, restoring our resources and managing the factors that lead to too much pressure. Which brings us to handling stress.

HANDLING STRESS

To handle stress, first and foremost you need to know that you're stressed. This might sound simple or even silly, but I cannot tell you how often our body is under tension that our distracted mind doesn't register. There's an overlap here in that our mindfulness practices – yoga, meditation and micro-meditations – from the last chapter are the obvious first antidote in this arena too. We have to learn to sense the signals of internal tension through enhanced bodily awareness to be able to remedy them. Our stress response is controlled by our autonomic nervous system, which has two settings: sympathetic (fight or flight) and parasympathetic (rest and digest). Switching off one switches on the other. So when we talk about a healthy stress response, we are talking about fluctuating between these two settings.

To sense when our body has switched into the sympathetic system, we can bring awareness to the following sensations, which will increase in their intensity as the stressful state persists. These are the hallmarks of the fight or flight response:

- Dry eyes (which over time often lead to the infamous 'stress twitch')
- Dry mouth
- Sweating (often with a distinct odour)
- Increased heart rate or palpitations
- Digestive discomfort/bloating/constipation (as the body's digestive function is inhibited in this state)
- Hypervigilance/focus on danger and threat/negative rumination/disrupted mood
- Decreased libido or sexual functioning
- Disrupted sleep/insomnia

Back in 2017, when I was in the fast lane to burnout, even when I could sense a growing internal tension, I didn't know how to fix it in the short or long term. Stress is cumulative; relaxation is not. I'll repeat that, just to fully emphasise how important it is: *stress is cumulative; relaxation is not*! Stress and tension build steadily, unconsciously, without any effort at all. Like a slowly dripping tap partial to the odd outpouring, day after day tensions become habitual – our new normal – which is partially why this simmering, low-grade state becomes so difficult to detect. To mitigate growing stress and tension we *have* to make a consistent, conscious, daily effort to practise bodily awareness followed by some of the following techniques to downshift the sympathetic nervous system. Because just as illness and distress are often brought about by the accumulation of lots of little tensions, vitality and wellness can be brought about by the practice of little relaxations.

TEN TOOLS TO DISRUPT THE ACCUMULATION OF STRESS, IN JUST 60 SECONDS

These techniques, based on the work of Andrew Goliszek and the 60-second stress management method, should discharge building tension without straining the body. You, of course, do not have to use them all – just take what works for you and leave what doesn't. It's important to have a few that you can use anywhere, anytime, at the first awareness of tension in the body, mental or physical.

○ Body focus

Close your eyes and bring your attention to your body – sense where your body is in contact with the environment around you (a chair, the floor, etc.). Bring your attention to an area of tension in the body (clenched jaw, raised shoulders, tension in the lower back, etc.). Breathe in, and on the exhale imagine that place loosening up. Then gently and slowly move that part of the body. Repeat for 60 seconds.

○ Using the breath

Breathe in through the nose (making sure the breath expands your belly and doesn't stop in your chest) and out through the mouth for each of these variables.

- **Strengthening breath 4-6-8:**
  Inhale for a count of 4, hold for a count of 6, exhale for a count of 8, pause with emptied lungs before the next inhale.

- **Basic breath 4 × 4:**
  Inhale for a count of 4, exhale for a count of 4, pause with emptied lungs before the next inhale.

- **Relaxing breath 4 × 8:**
  Inhale for a count of 4, exhale for a count of 8, pause with emptied lungs before the next inhale.

Repeat whichever breathwork technique you like anywhere from 5 to 10 times. These are especially useful tools to apply after sudden stress to prevent tension setting into the body.

○ Yawning

Let the yawn last as long as you can, which naturally elongates your exhalation. It sounds odd, but it works – simply making our exhalation longer than our inhalation downregulates the body's stress response.

○ Neck stretches and shoulder rolls

Move your head left and right, gently stretching your neck, then down to your chest and in slow circles in one direction and then the other direction. While you're doing this, try to place the spotlight of your attention on your breath – just feel the breath enter and leave your body without any effort on your part.

With your hands on your lap, firmly but slowly circle your shoulders forwards and then backwards. Do 10 to 20 rolls, then relax and finish by shrugging a few times.

○ Eye stretches and palming

Close your eyes, then move them in slow circles one way, relax, and then the other way. Rub your palms together until they warm, then place them over your eyes, cupping them gently, not applying pressure. Feel the warmth and let your eyes relax for a few moments. Blink your eyes gently back open.

○ The voo technique

This is based on the work of somatic experiencing expert Peter Levine, PhD. Start by inhaling deeply into the belly and on the exhalation (with a deep foghorn voice) make the sound 'voooooo' until the lungs are fully emptied. It feels strange at first but, I promise, it's a very effective means of inducing calm.

○ Apple-picker stretch

Standing with both arms in the air and gently bouncing on the tips of your toes, reach as high as you can, then gently bend over towards the floor as far as is comfortable, with knees slightly bent. Sway gently from side to side for a few moments before rising up slowly, one vertebra at a time, with your neck and head unwinding last.

Set peace of mind as your highest goal and organise your life around it.

— BRIAN TRACY

○ Body tapping

This technique comes from the work of neuropsychiatrist Dr Dan Siegel. Using the palms and fingers, start to gently tap (or slap) your arms, the sides of your torso, down your legs and back up your body. Use your right arm to tap the left side of your body and your left arm to tap the right side. Continue for 60 seconds.

○ Lion prune face

Take a deep breath and stretch your face muscles as far as they will go, at the same time opening your eyes wide and sticking your tongue out as far as it will go. Then close your eyes tight and tightly press your lips together while tightening your face muscles, then relax. Again, it sounds odd, but it works!

○ Arm shakes

Standing with your arms by your sides, start to shake your hands and wrists. Let the movement continue up through the elbows and into the upper arms until your whole arms are shaking (fairly vigorously). Continue to shake your arms until you reach 60 seconds, then relax. You can also do this exercise on your legs, one at a time.

As simple as these techniques sound, the growing body of research to support them is robust.[9] Use any you like for just 60 seconds to interrupt stress and tension in the body. They are most effective when woven regularly into our daily lives, becoming our tension-busting habits. As they become more habitual, you can begin to use them in conjunction with a distinct focus on the breath for the duration of the 60 seconds (of course, with the exception of 'using the breath' and 'the voo technique', as you'll already be doing so).

Here are two additional tools – and two of my absolute favourites – both of which are enormously powerful stress relievers, but require slightly more than 60 seconds:

∘ Dancing

Dance is found in every culture in the world and there's a very good reason why. Movement discharges stress and tension, helps with emotional integration and releases lots of feel-good hormones. After a tough day, in the privacy of your own space, turn on your favourite music and move!

∘ Earthing

Simply walking barefoot on the earth can have a profound effect on our internal experience, allowing us not only a respite from stress and tension, but also the many benefits of bathing in nature and rebalancing our body with the earth's harmonising electrons.[10]

When you feel stress building in the body or mind, try one or more of these quick and easy techniques to help discharge tension, then in your own time you could take a moment to journal through the following questions:

- What does my body need right now?
- What expectations are unrealistic in this moment?
- What boundaries do I need to set or adjust?
- What changes could I make right now?
- What are the things I cannot control?
- What am I thankful for right now?
- What brings me meaning and purpose?
- What support system (friends, family, community, therapist) could I turn to?

GUIDED RELAXATION

During my own journey from intense burnout back to well-being, I spent years educating myself on what happened to me, how and why it happened and how I could begin to help others experiencing the same thing. I have since returned to college to study for my psychotherapy degree and have started a company called The STLL – for now it is an online resource – to empower those on their own journey. On The STLL (www.thestll.com) you will find downloadable guided yoga and meditation courses and a wonderful community of people who, through our shared online and in-person events, will help you to master breathwork, movement, contemplative practices and stress management tools. There are informative articles explaining why we do this work and the many benefits there to be reaped. Plus there are free-to-access 10–20-minute guided relaxation techniques provided by the Stress Management Institute of Ireland and voiced by the company director and founder of Resilience International Ray McKiernan, among them:

○ Progressive muscle relaxation

This behavioural therapy method helps people to cope with the stresses of daily living. Its main function is to achieve voluntary mental and physical relaxation, but it is also a somatic tool which helps with interoception (sensing our inner world). This practice is very effective and easily learned.

○ Visualisation

Some people think predominantly in language, others in imagery. This practice can be a good entry relaxation technique for those with who think largely in images or those with a particularly busy mind. Engaging the visualisation capacities of the right brain-hemisphere quiets the mental chatter of the left brain-hemisphere.

○ Autogenic relaxation

This is a guided somatic experience which systematically focuses attention down through every muscle group in the body. This practice strengthens the mind–body connection with the use of sensory imagination, like feelings of heat or heaviness.

○ Sound meditation

This synchronises brain waves to achieve profound states of relaxation and helps to restore the normal vibratory frequencies of the cells in our bodies. This might sound new-age, but the adult body is 75 per cent water and water is a great conductor of sound vibrations. The sound wave is heard through the ear, passing through the auditory nerve, then the vagus nerve, stimulating every organ in the body. We already instinctually understand this process – just think about how your favourite song can lift your mood. Certain instruments, like chimes, are particularly powerful for sound meditation.

These guided relaxation techniques are brilliant additional tools in our daily, conscious efforts to create relaxation in the body, and they can be used whenever you feel like it.

SELF-CARE PRACTICES AND A LIFESTYLE APPROACH

In *Jump*, as a buffer against anxiety and mounting stress, I also mentioned self-care practices like:

- A walk in nature (something we'll discuss in much greater detail in Chapter 8, 'The Science of Awe and Gratitude')
- Massage
- Acupuncture
- Reiki
- Sensory deprivation float tanks
- Reflexology
- A pedicure!

Self-care is whatever creates a sense of total relaxation or release in the body and/or mind. Self-care is not a luxury: it is a necessary refuelling of our internal resources against the very real assault of stressors that we face day in, day out. We should indulge ourselves in relaxation and self-care practices often and without guilt. They are what will allow us to continue to function and perform at our best over prolonged periods of time.

Beyond these tools, to thoroughly manage our lifelong stress a lifestyle approach is necessary – this focuses on a combination of areas to create an overall strengthening of reserve energies and stamina that generally leads to an ability to bounce back from stress. So in addition to breathwork and 60-second exercises, guided relaxation techniques and general self-care practices, we could also work to develop healthy habits in these aspects of our life:

- Diet and nutrition
- Exercise
- Sleep hygiene
- Social support and connection
- Humour and play

Predictability

Research suggests that the most challenging qualities of any stressors are ambiguity, unpredictability and uncontrollability. One important stress management strategy is to develop the ability to notice when these qualities are present. Then create as much predictability as possible by clarifying details or reducing the amount of time you spend with ambiguous or unmanageable demands.

YOUR 7-DAY STRESS DIARY CHALLENGE

In light of everything we've discussed about stress throughout this chapter, I hope this exercise will bring insight and useful new habits. For the next seven days, focus on mastering the art of getting to know, understand and modulate your unique stress-response triggers. Using the template provided, fill in your stress diary at the end of every day. It's always best to pick one area and work on it for a while until it's mastered. Of course, adjust it to your situation, trial and test the different techniques and practices, but do try to stick to the recommendations to get maximum benefits and integration of this new skill. Sometimes it can take months for a new behaviour to become automatic, so constant practice is essential because repetition is the foundation of change and habit creation. Be patient with yourself but also try to be disciplined. The goal is to develop progress with your stress management, not perfection. I've filled out one sample diary.

SAMPLE STRESS DIARY

TIME/DAY	Wednesday, midday.
EVENT	I had an upcoming annual review in work, made worse by my uncompleted workload on our latest project and my boss recently giving me ambiguous feedback.
HOW YOU FELT FROM 1 TO 10	Very stressed and expecting the worst, about a 7.5.
PHYSICAL SYMPTOMS	No appetite, jittery, shallow breathing, brain fog, dry mouth, muscle tension.
AUTOMATIC THOUGHTS	I was anticipating and imagining a bad review and receiving unimpressed feedback. I was further dreading having to talk to my colleagues after the review and having to come into the office tomorrow.
INTERVENTION	I did 60 seconds of relaxing breath and body focus, then I found a quiet space and did a further 60 seconds of the voo technique. I considered alternative outcomes to my automatic negative thoughts and offered myself some words of genuine compassion and support.
HOW YOU FELT AFTER INTERVENTION	Much better, still a little apprehensive for my review but I felt more ready and capable of handling any constructive criticism, around a 4.

STRESS DIARY: DAY I

TIME/DAY	
EVENT	
HOW YOU FELT FROM I TO IO	
PHYSICAL SYMPTOMS	
AUTOMATIC THOUGHTS	
INTERVENTION	
HOW YOU FELT AFTER INTERVENTION	

STRESS DIARY: DAY 2

TIME/DAY	
EVENT	
HOW YOU FELT FROM 1 TO 10	
PHYSICAL SYMPTOMS	
AUTOMATIC THOUGHTS	
INTERVENTION	
HOW YOU FELT AFTER INTERVENTION	

STRESS DIARY: DAY 3

TIME/DAY	
EVENT	
HOW YOU FELT FROM 1 TO 10	
PHYSICAL SYMPTOMS	
AUTOMATIC THOUGHTS	
INTERVENTION	
HOW YOU FELT AFTER INTERVENTION	

STRESS DIARY: DAY 4

TIME/DAY	
EVENT	
HOW YOU FELT FROM 1 TO 10	
PHYSICAL SYMPTOMS	
AUTOMATIC THOUGHTS	
INTERVENTION	
HOW YOU FELT AFTER INTERVENTION	

STRESS DIARY: DAY 5

TIME/DAY	
EVENT	
HOW YOU FELT FROM 1 TO 10	
PHYSICAL SYMPTOMS	
AUTOMATIC THOUGHTS	
INTERVENTION	
HOW YOU FELT AFTER INTERVENTION	

STRESS DIARY: DAY 6

TIME/DAY	
EVENT	
HOW YOU FELT FROM I TO IO	
PHYSICAL SYMPTOMS	
AUTOMATIC THOUGHTS	
INTERVENTION	
HOW YOU FELT AFTER INTERVENTION	

STRESS DIARY: DAY 7

TIME/DAY	
EVENT	
HOW YOU FELT FROM 1 TO 10	
PHYSICAL SYMPTOMS	
AUTOMATIC THOUGHTS	
INTERVENTION	
HOW YOU FELT AFTER INTERVENTION	

chapter 6

core personal values

'Your beliefs become your thoughts,
Your thoughts become your words,
Your words become your actions,
Your actions become your habits,
Your habits become your values,
Your values become your destiny.'

— GANDHI

The first time I read about personal values I was 30 and on a layover in Taiwan. Four months earlier I had moved to Mexico's paradise, the Yucatán Peninsula, to live with my boyfriend, whom I'd met while backpacking through Central and South America – you'll know the full and truly magical story if you've read *Jump*. But my fairy-tale ending had not materialised at all as it had promised, nor as I had become so attached to envisioning. He had dumped me. So with the poison of rejection eroding my sense of self-worth and confidence, I'd packed my entire life into two giant suitcases and booked a flight alone from Cancún to Bali. Sitting in that airport was about as lost as I'd ever felt in my adult life. No job, no home, no plan, a rapidly dwindling savings account, an absolutely shattered heart to accompany the still lingering sting of that catastrophic burnout, and only these two giant, unmanageable suitcases to accompany me on my aimless roaming. In a desperate attempt at self-empowerment I had downloaded a Tony Robbins book to my Kindle for the day-long journey across the globe, and suddenly the idea of tapping into some kind of internal safety net sounded very appealing. He was talking about core personal values.

In the Oxford English Dictionary, 'values' are defined as: 'Principles or standards of behaviour; one's judgement on what is important in life'. If we don't know our values, we don't know ourselves. Every life coach, spiritual guru, wellness mogul or trained therapist the world over understands this simple fact. When our lives are entirely run by our unpredictable feelings and emotions, or our even more unpredictable circumstances, we will always be in some state of chaos, uncertainty or discomfort, mentally, physically or emotionally. A highly developed values system is like a compass. It serves as a guide to point us in the right direction when we feel lost or when life gets overwhelming. When we honour what it is that we value, the good days become even more fulfilling and on the bad days we can navigate life's unrelenting challenges from a place of steady personal integrity.

DISCOVER YOUR CORE PERSONAL VALUES

It sounds so simple, but most of us don't know our values. We don't understand what is truly important to us as individuals. Instead, we'll often default to what it is our family, our community, our culture or our mainstream media values as a reliable answer for ourselves. It's easy to speculate or imagine what we *should* value. But knowing and accepting what it is we *actually* value takes a little effort and a process of discovery. This process is best undertaken with an open mind, a lot of honesty and a little patience. Remember that our conscious mind does not have all the answers – it is only the very tip of the iceberg of who we are. To allow ourselves access to the less obvious truths, we simply have to recognise that fact, release our preconceived ideas and come to this process with curiosity, with a willingness to learn something new about ourselves.

To help you uncover your core personal values, I'll walk you through a four-step process.

° STEP I – creating your 'master values' list

We will work through four exercises to create this list.

Exercise 1: peak experiences

Consider an important or meaningful moment that stands out to you.

- What were you doing?
  I was hiking through Patagonia after being told it was an impossible feat.

- What was going on around you?
  I was surrounded by nature, new friends and feeling completely awestruck.

- What values were you honouring at the time?
  Utter freedom.

What were you doing?

_____

_____

_____

What was going on around you?

_____

_____

_____

What values were you honouring at the time?

_____

_____

_____

Exercise 2: suppressed values

Consider a time when you felt angry, frustrated or upset.

- What was going on?
  I was exhausted, overworked and on the verge of burnout.

- What were you feeling?
  Emotionally unstable, irritable, ungrateful and generally miserable.

- Now flip those feelings around. What value was being suppressed?
  My health and wellbeing, and a simple life I could actually enjoy.

What was going on?

_____

_____

_____

What were you feeling?

_____

_____

_____

What value was being suppressed?

_____

_____

_____

Exercise 3: code of conduct

Beyond your basic human needs, what *must* you have in your life to experience happiness and fulfilment? What are the personal values you must honour or a part of you wilts? For example:

- *Creative expression*
- *Health and vitality*
- *Excitement and adventure*
- *Beautiful surroundings*
- *New knowledge and learning*

_____

_____

_____

_____

_____

_____

_____

Exercise 4: resonant values

At first I was reluctant to share a list of values because scanning a list like this can cause our minds to look for the next value that exceeds the last. In other words, we may end up choosing values based on our desired self-image rather than our truth. Our values are supposed to reveal themselves to us over time as we increase our self-awareness – and that will happen naturally as a part of this bigger journey we're on – but in the name of efficacy (and because I personally found this really insightful when defining my own) I have put together a list of over 200 values. As you read through this list, highlight every value that resonates with you, being mindful of self-honesty as you do.

Acceptance	Carefulness	Contribution
Accomplishment	Certainty	Control
Accountability	Challenge	Conviction
Accuracy	Charity	Cooperation
Achievement	Cleanliness	Courage
Adaptability	Clearness	Courtesy
Alertness	Cleverness	Creation
Altruism	Comfort	Creativity
Ambition	Commitment	Credibility
Amusement	Common sense	Curiosity
Assertiveness	Communication	Decisiveness
Attentiveness	Community	Dedication
Awareness	Compassion	Dependability
Balance	Competence	Determination
Beauty	Concentration	Development
Boldness	Confidence	Devotion
Bravery	Connection	Dignity
Brilliance	Conscientiousness	Discipline
Calmness	Consciousness	Discovery
Candour	Consistency	Drive
Capability	Contentment	Effectiveness

Efficiency	Generosity	Intelligence
Empathy	Genius	Intensity
Empowerment	Giving	Intuitiveness
Endurance	Goodness	Joy
Energy	Grace	Justice
Enjoyment	Gratitude	Kindness
Enthusiasm	Greatness	Knowledge
Equality	Growth	Lawfulness
Ethicalness	Happiness	Leadership
Excellence	Hard work	Learning
Experience	Harmony	Liberty
Exploration	Health	Logic
Expressiveness	Honesty	Love
Fairness	Honour	Loyalty
Fame	Hopefulness	Mastery
Family	Humility	Maturity
Fearlessness	Humour	Meaning
Feelings	Imagination	Moderation
Ferociousness	Improvement	Motivation
Fidelity	Independence	Openness
Focus	Individuality	Optimism
Foresight	Innovation	Order
Fortitude	Inquisitiveness	Organisation
Freedom	Insightfulness	Originality
Friendship	Inspiration	Passion
Fun	Integrity	Patience

Peace	Security	Teamwork
Performance	Self-reliance	Temperance
Persistence	Selflessness	Thankfulness
Playfulness	Sensitivity	Thoroughness
Poise	Serenity	Thoughtfulness
Potential	Service	Timeliness
Power	Sharing	Tolerance
Presentness	Significance	Toughness
Productivity	Silence	Tradition
Professionalism	Simplicity	Tranquillity
Prosperity	Sincerity	Transparency
Purpose	Skilfulness	Trustworthiness
Quality	Smartness	Truth
Realism	Solitude	Understanding
Reason	Spirituality	Uniqueness
Recognition	Spontaneity	Unity
Recreation	Stability	Valour
Reflectiveness	Status	Victory
Respect	Stewardship	Vigour
Responsibility	Strength	Vision
Restraint	Structure	Vitality
Results	Success	Wealth
Reverence	Support	Welcoming
Rigour	Surprise	Winning
Risk	Sustainability	Wisdom
Satisfaction	Talent	Wonder

° STEP 2 – categorise your values and highlight the central theme of each grouping

Combine your answers from each exercise in Step 1 to create your 'master list' of values. If you're anything like me, that could be upwards of 40 values written and highlighted, which is way too many to have any actionable meaning to you just yet.

Values like accountability, responsibility and timeliness are related. Learning, growth and development all relate to each other too. Connection, belonging and intimacy – you see what I'm getting at? Here we'll group our master list values into related themes:

_____

_____

_____

_____

_____

_____

_____

_____

_____

_____

_____

_____

_____

_____

_____

_____

Now with all your values grouped, select a primary value which highlights the central theme of each group. You don't need to get rid of any of the other values in the group, just choose a word that best represents that grouping. For example, if you have a group of values that includes 'honesty', 'transparency', 'integrity', 'directness' and 'truth', perhaps 'integrity' might be the umbrella word you choose to capture all the values listed.

_____

_____

_____

_____

_____

_____

_____

○ STEP 3 – determine your top core personal values in order of their importance

Now for the hardest part. While examining your primary value from each grouping, ask yourself the following questions:

- What values are essential to my life?
- What values represent my primary way of being?
- What values are essential to supporting my inner self?

Your core personal values are what matter most to you when no one is watching. Ideally, we would end up with a list of at least 5 but no more than 10. This is enough to capture the complex and unique dimensions of who you are while still allowing you to remember your core values and put them to use for you.

_____

_____

_____

_____

_____

_____

_____

And we're not quite finished yet! Once you have your master list whittled down to no more than 10 values, rank them in their order of importance to you. You may need to do this in multiple sittings. Rank them, sleep on it and revisit it tomorrow to see how it feels to you with fresh eyes. Play with this ranking until you're happy.

_____

_____

_____

_____

_____

_____

_____

We want to give our values life, make them emotional and
meaningful to us so we are inspired to uphold them. We can
use other values from our earlier groupings in Step 2 to describe
and enrich our top values here. For example:

1. *Freedom: to live a life full of adventure, exploration
   and boldness. To be unique and spontaneous. To
   discover all the awe, wonder and inspiration the world
   has to offer.*
2. *Love: commitment to family, friends and a partner.
   For me, this means a life filled with respect, loyalty,
   gratitude, trust and support.*
3. *Health/wellbeing: to live with passion, vitality and
   optimism every day.*
4. *Learning: for self-development, growth, purpose,
   prosperity and wisdom.*
5. *Communication: for creative expression, authenticity,
   openness and a sense of contribution.*
6. *Simplicity: for peace, calm and contentment. For
   humility, solitude and self-awareness.*
7. *Beauty: to cultivate a life of beauty and awe inside,
   outside and all around. Inside for confidence, kindness,
   compassion and self-respect, outside for the expression
   of my inner capacity, and all around me in the beauty
   of the natural world I choose to inhabit.*

Enrich your top values with statements that make them mean-ingful to you:

_____

_____

_____

_____

_____

_____

_____

_____

_____

_____

_____

_____

_____

_____

_____

_____

_____

_____

_____

_____

_____

_____

_____

_____

_____

_____

_____

Once you have done all this work, revisit your list of meaningful personal values ranked in the order you chose for review. Ask yourself:

- How do they make me feel?
- Are they consistent with who I am?
- Are they personal to me?
- Do any of my values feel inconsistent with my identity, as if they belong to someone else?
- Are my values in the proper order of importance?

There's no need to overthink this process because nothing is final here. These are the foundation blocks of your highly developed values system, and as new values reveal themselves to you, as you grow in self-awareness and life experience, your list will change – perhaps only in priority or perhaps altogether. Tweaks and changes can be made as necessary; only your awareness needs to remain key and consistent.

MAKING VALUES-BASED DECISIONS

Once you are clear on your values at this moment, you can step back and assess whether you're honouring these values in your life at this time too. We won't always be able to honour *all* our values simultaneously. For instance, I consciously decided to restrict my freedom for four years to return to college to honour my value of learning. It's about understanding and accepting ourselves, knowing what matters most to us and what a good life means to us. When we have this knowledge we can make *values-based decisions*. This is one of the greatest skills you can give yourself for *all* life's crossroads, twists and turns.

Of course, there will always be exceptions, occasions when our decisions will involve a conflict between two or more of our core personal values. But as a general rule of thumb:

- Knowing, accepting and honouring our values can make decision-making easy. There is far less ambiguity, self-doubt and rumination – it's a simple yes or no as to whether this path aligns with our core personal values, or what matters most to us. If not, it's probably not a path we want to follow.

- Knowing, accepting and honouring our individual values is authenticity unmatched. It gives us a robust sense of fulfilment. It is living life on our own terms.

- Knowing, accepting and honouring our values means that we stay faithful to ourselves rather than betraying ourselves in search of approval or any other external source of validation.

- Knowing, accepting and honouring our values allows us to recognise when something or someone in our life is out of sync with those principles. That internal dissonance, the gut feeling we sometimes get in these scenarios, can be examined against our value system and understood.

- Knowing, accepting and honouring our values sets the stage for who we want to be and how we want to move through the world. When we give action to our values, we not only live in alignment with who we truly are, we also set ourselves up for success on our own terms.

- Knowing, accepting and honouring our values is how we build character, self-respect and integrity. It's just an added bonus that this is often recognised by others too.

- Knowing, accepting and honouring our values allows us to transcend the belief structures we've internalised from our parental and cultural conditioning – which brings us smoothly and seamlessly to our next chapter, 'Self-Limiting Beliefs and Negative Self-Talk'.

Time to

MINDFULLY SELF-REFLECT AND BRING AWARENESS TO OUR EXPERIENCE

Before moving on, you may want to take a moment to bring your awareness to how you're feeling after working through this chapter, always paying attention to any resistance. Pause, take a deep grounding breath and focus your attention inwards.

Using your growing self-awareness and self-understanding, jot down whatever comes to mind – any feelings, thoughts, emotions or sensations triggered by this chapter's work.

_____

_____

_____

_____

_____

_____

_____

_____

_____

_____

_____

_____

_____

_____

_____

_____

_____

_____

_____

_____

_____

_____

_____

_____

_____

self-limiting beliefs and negative self-talk

'Why do you stay in prison
when the door is wide open?'
— RUMI

SELF-LIMITING BELIEFS

Our beliefs are acquired from our interpretation of all our past experiences. Put simply, a belief is a thought that is true for you. We each have hundreds, even thousands, of beliefs, all working to create and maintain our reality as we understand it. What we see, what we hear, what we think, what we imagine, what inspires us – all of this comes from our beliefs, and our brains constantly seek and find evidence to continue supporting them. As a species, we're generally not very good at changing to accommodate novel information, preferring to slightly bend reality instead to fit our existing worldview. In this way, our experiences often become feedback loops, reinforcing our beliefs again and again. A self-fulfilling prophecy: what we expect is what we receive. Our beliefs really are powerful invisible mental prisons that create the world we experience every day. If you've ever tried to argue with someone who has a dissimilar belief, you'll also know first-hand how adamantly we defend them, good or bad.

To demonstrate the influence of our beliefs in a fascinating way, consider this experiment, conducted by Blakemore and Cooper in 1970 (when ethical standards and animal welfare were far less of a research concern). Two special cylindrical spaces were created, one with only vertical lines inside and the other with only horizontal lines inside. Newborn kittens were placed into one of the two cylindrical spaces for the first few months of their lives and otherwise cared for as normal. The only variable was that one kitten was never exposed to any horizontal lines in their environment, while the other was never exposed to any vertical lines in their environment. Once they were placed into a normal space, kittens that only perceived vertical lines for the first few months of life could no longer see horizontal lines that existed in their reality, and vice versa. They would walk right into chairs or off the edges of high tabletops, completely blind to these objects or transitions that conflicted with the beliefs they had created about what exists in an environment. This impairment persisted for the rest of their lives. Scientific research has done some cruel things in pursuit of compelling insight.

What this experiment tells us is that many of the realities we perceive are a socially constructed illusion based on a complex set of beliefs. This is a humbling and liberating truth all at once. Since I learned this explicitly, I have never been able to argue that I'm absolutely right about anything, nor have I been able to fully believe all the stories in my head. Our unconscious beliefs and the realities we build with them give us our imaginary limitations or our endless possibilities. And once again, it is self-reflection and self-awareness that allow us to go beyond the conditioning of our minds here – an ability those poor kittens didn't possess. When we consciously change our beliefs – or the stories that we tell ourselves about ourselves – we change our worlds! It's really that simple. But to do this we first need to become aware of the voice inside our head that chatters incessantly.

The average person has over 60,000 thoughts daily – that's approximately 41 thoughts per minute – most of which fall outside of or just below conscious awareness. An *enormous* 90 per cent of these 60,000 daily thoughts are repetitive and automatic, which is the reason they fall outside of conscious awareness – like breathing or riding a bicycle, they no longer require your attention or effort to circulate. It's easy to see how repetition of this nature can become blindly embedded as a rigid belief – the more you tell yourself something, the more you believe it. To address the self-limiting beliefs that run in an infinite loop in our minds, we have to shine the spotlight of awareness on them.

To give you some guidance (or perhaps permission) to tap into this wounded part of yourself, let me share my first ever list of self-limiting beliefs. This was written during my first year of psychotherapy training, when I believed I had done a lot of work on self-love, self-development and self-acceptance. Yet on active inspection, I discovered these negative thoughts still whirled in my head daily:

- 'My nose makes me so ugly'
- 'People don't like me'
- 'If I am not busy/successful I am worthless'
- 'My career defines me'
- 'Big negative emotions are not acceptable'
- 'I am not important enough/deserving/worthy of X'
- 'I will never meet anyone to share my life with'
- 'All men will lose interest in me, cheat on me and/or leave me eventually'
- 'I have to be 100 per cent self-sufficient – nothing less is good enough'
- 'I will never have enough money'
- 'I can't do/I'm no good at X'
- 'I'm getting old'
- 'I'm getting fat'
- 'People think I'm annoying/stupid/a bitch'

- 'I am not a good friend'
- 'I am never heard/understood'

This is just a small selection of the barely conscious racket that I managed to tap into in various contexts.

IDENTIFYING YOUR SELF-LIMITING BELIEFS

Here are some tricks to help you identify your self-limiting beliefs.

○ Look for an incongruence

This is a stark difference between how you feel and what is actually happening. For instance, your new relationship is going well, but instead of feeling happy and at ease, you feel worried and uneasy. This is a red flag for a limiting belief at play, and when you pay closer attention to your inner experience, you might be telling yourself something like 'This is too good to be true', 'I don't deserve this' or 'I'm only allowed so much happiness until something terrible happens'.

○ Look at your parents

Whether or not we like it, we often inherit the limiting beliefs of our parents. Ask yourself questions like:

1. What fears did your parent(s) have when you were growing up?
2. Did your parents give you any direct or implicit messaging around what it means to be a man/woman, money, marriage and so on?

3. What were you praised for by your parents growing up? What were you judged for?

4. Did you modify your behaviour/coping skills for more praise? Less criticism?

○ Fill in the blank

This is a simple but effective technique. Describe a situation that you don't like about your life – something you're struggling with or have struggled with (paying particular attention to your repeated or pattern struggles). Add 'because' to the end of the description and then finish the sentence aloud without overthinking – say whatever first comes to mind. For example, 'I can't start my own business *because* I don't have enough money.' Your limiting belief here is scarcity around money.

○ Spot the defence mechanisms

Think back to Chapter 3, 'Navigating Conflict', and our list of defence mechanisms (flick back to page 58 to refresh your memory if you need to). These defence mechanisms show up energetically and with *vigour* to guard our beliefs! It could be an interesting thought experiment to ask yourself:

• Is there truth for me in the exact opposite of what I'm feeling?

• Am I defending myself against facing that feeling?

EXAMINING YOUR SELF-LIMITING BELIEFS

Take *at least* 10 minutes, and longer if needed, to really focus on the negative, doubtful, self-sabotaging things you say to yourself on repeat. Be radically honest and allow whatever surfaces to be written down without editing or explanation: write it exactly as you speak it to yourself – even if it sounds childish or triggers an uncomfortable sense of shame, sadness, irritation and so on. In fact, if it does either of those things you have *definitely* cracked the shell of a limiting belief, so give yourself a pat on the back.

_____

_____

_____

_____

_____

_____

_____

_____

_____

_____

_____

_____

_____

_____

Update this list over the coming days, weeks or even months as you come to recognise new limiting beliefs surfacing for you in various contexts. The more we bring awareness to them, the more we can change and heal them.

With the list of your self-limiting beliefs in front of you, scan what you've written and see if the origin of any of your repetitive thoughts comes to mind immediately. For instance, referring back to my own list here, when I was very young, maybe five or six years old, I had an accident on a bicycle with my dad. My foot got stuck in the spokes of the front wheel, the bike flipped, he broke his shoulder, requiring metal plate surgery, and I took the full impact on my nose. I have hated my nose since, subconsciously (and often consciously) telling myself I was ugly as a result of it. With this thought and its related low self-confidence looping in my mind since age five or six, it inevitably seeped into every area of my life from work to relationships, affecting things I never could have imagined until I brought awareness to it and began to notice how often it was the fundamental belief structure at play, buried under various feelings and expressions. Bear in mind, experiences from our formative years, from birth to age seven, will be particularly relevant here.

You will find that some self-limiting beliefs have clear origins, like that one, while others will be linked directly to your feelings of self-esteem, which we already know is a universal core psychological challenge for all humans. If you related most to

Group 5 or **Group 6** in the exercise from Chapter 2 on identifying your core psychological challenges, pay close attention for issues of self-esteem looping in your limiting beliefs. The obvious ones on my list are 'People don't like me' and 'I'm not important enough/deserving/worthy of X'. You will also spot conflicts in your subconscious messaging, as you can see with my 'I will never meet anyone to share my life with' and 'I have to be 100 per cent self-sufficient – nothing less is good enough'. These are great insights to learn about yourself. And you will generally find when it comes to these conflicted beliefs that one is your authentic, vulnerable truth while the other is the protective measure or defence against it. My fear is that I will never meet anyone to share my life with, so instead I will demand a busy, successful, 100 per cent self-sufficient version of myself, and nothing less is good enough. How ironic that one belief impinges so distinctly on the realisation of another.

As well as issues of self-esteem, vulnerability and fear, you will also see themes emerging from childhood like 'I'm never heard/understood', themes of scarcity, shame, self-doubt, self-sabotage and even self-loathing. The other universal core psychological challenges of bearing need and dependency and managing intense emotion may also appear.

Take a moment to once again examine your own list of self-limiting beliefs for similar themes. Consider where these thoughts may have come from, what may underlie them and how they are connected. When you read through your list, ask yourself if any of these sound like the words of a parent or another significant person in your life, past or present? Try to really get under the surface of each belief that circulates for you, and try to find its roots. It is often something surprisingly simple and linked back to our inner child.

REMEDYING SELF-LIMITING BELIEFS

If we want to create lasting change in our lives, we *have to* let go of our self-limiting beliefs and cultivate an empowering self-image that supports our growth and brings awareness to the endless possibilities available to us. In other words, we need to repeatedly tell ourselves better stories. This sounds simple but it is truly life-altering work.

○ Disempower the inner critic by giving them a name

I have named my inner critic Sally. Now any time I become aware of one of my old limiting scripts doing the rounds in my head, I know immediately that it's not my story: it's that absolute weapon Sally back to try to ruin the day.

Name your inner critic here: _____

○ Pay close attention to when the inner critic arises

Has something or someone in your environment triggered this familiar thought pattern? Having examined your common self-limiting beliefs, can you dig below the mental chatter to the emotion it signifies? Perhaps the trigger in your environment has actually made you feel shame, anger, a sense of being overwhelmed, fear or inadequacy. But instead of perceiving the full weight of that awful emotion, your mind has instead surfaced the familiar self-sabotaging inner speech you've built around it. Can you begin to link the two and break the chain in the moment?

◦ Create opposing beliefs

To silence and reprogramme the inner critic we create opposing beliefs and think like a friend to ourselves. With the development of self-awareness, every time your inner critic surfaces with one of their repeat narratives, you want to have an arsenal of opposing beliefs to retaliate with. To build new habits we have to break the old ones. For these new opposing beliefs to have an impact on our inner critic we need to actually *believe* them. So the first step is to look for **facts and evidence** that indicate our inner critic is just plain wrong. For example:

- 'My nose makes me so ugly' becomes 'I worked for over ten years as a paid model; models are not ugly.'

This is a simple, objective fact. And even if I still undermined this fact in relation to myself at first, the sheer logic of it allowed me to slowly dissolve this long-held belief with repetition. Look for facts and evidence that directly dispute your limiting beliefs. These are very effective and work quickly.

However, there simply won't be facts to oppose all our beliefs, so next we apply **reason**. For example:

- 'People don't like me' becomes 'Nobody in this world is 100 per cent liked; not everyone is going to like me and that's okay.'
- 'All men will lose interest in me, cheat on me and/or leave me eventually' becomes 'Some men may lose interest in me but I trust myself and my intuition

to recognise what doesn't serve me and handle it
with grace.'

If you are struggling to apply reason or find plausible alternatives to your self-limiting beliefs, return to the ABC technique
on page 91 and apply it here.

Reason begins to soften the edges of our beliefs, allowing
us to start to shift them in the direction of believable positive and empowered stories. Some limiting beliefs are linked
to deep emotional wounds and we may have to reason with
ourselves around these for a while. But when it feels genuine
and authentic to you, you can start to tell yourself fully
opposing and uplifting stories in response to your inner critic.
For example:

- 'If I am not busy/successful I am worthless' becomes
  'My value and worth are intrinsic to me, just the way
  I am and without exception.'
- 'I will never meet anyone to share my life with' becomes
  'I love myself, my company and the life I am creating;
  I look forward to sharing my wonderful life with the
  right person.'
- 'I will never have enough money' becomes 'Money is
  just fun tickets – it flows to me in abundance.'
- 'I'm falling so far behind everyone else' becomes 'I am
  exactly where I am meant to be; my life is unfolding
  perfectly. I take great joy from every blessing and great
  growth from every challenge.'

DISCOVERING YOUR STRENGTHS OF CHARACTER

To aid you in reshaping your self-limiting beliefs into empowering stories, I want you to discover your signature strengths of character. Acknowledging and understanding the spectrum of positive traits that you carry with you as your birthright or that you have developed throughout your life is invaluable. Thankfully, there's a wonderful (and free) online resource to offer you this personalised wealth of uplifting self-awareness.

Google 'VIA Character Strengths Survey' and take the 15-minute survey on the VIA Institute on Character website. Note the results of your superpowers here. Please feel free to make your own additions to the list also.

Your strengths of character:

_____

_____

_____

_____

_____

_____

_____

_____

_____

_____

_____

_____

_____

Now having taken the time to really consider your worth, your wonderful traits and all the unique, interesting, passionate and compassionate qualities you embody and take with you into the world every day, write a factual or reasonable alternative and/or a truly empowering opposing belief for every self-limiting belief you made a note of earlier:

The greatest sources of our suffering are the lies we tell ourselves

— BESSEL VAN DER KOLK

COMMUNICATING WITH OURSELVES

We all know that communication skills are vital for success, but something we rarely consider is that this includes how we communicate with ourselves. On my own journey back to wellbeing and self-love I learned the undeniable power of our inner language and how often we let ourselves down in this regard, speaking to ourselves in ways we would never dream of speaking to anyone else. Beyond our inner critic limiting us with rigid and repetitive beliefs, more generalised negative self-talk makes us procrastinate, compare ourselves with others, excessively self-blame, ruminate, worry and fret. I'm not suggesting we need to aspire towards some kind of inner utopia where there is only sunshine and rainbows – far from it. I'm a big advocate of constructive self-reflection and self-motivation. However, there's a big difference between **intentional** self-criticism and **habitual** self-criticism. One actively pursues growth; the other unknowingly stunts it.

Intentional self-criticism sounds like: 'I know I can do better in this area and I will endeavour to do so for my own greater good and the benefit of all those around me.'

Habitual self-criticism sounds like: 'I'm not good enough and I'll never be good enough. This is how things will always be.'

There are four types of self-talk – instructional, motivational, positive and negative.

- Instructional self-talk

Instructional self-talk happens when we guide ourselves through a task. It might sound like: 'To start the car I need to slowly press the accelerator while simultaneously releasing the clutch.'

- Motivational self-talk

Motivational self-talk is usually used to evaluate and step up to a challenge. It might sound like: 'I have prepared well for this speech – I know I can do it. I will channel any anxious feelings into excitement because I cannot wait to share my knowledge with those listening. I will do the best I can do.'

- Positive self-talk

Positive self-talk is your internal narrative about yourself. It might sound like: 'Even though it wasn't the outcome I had hoped for, I learned a lot about myself from the experience.'

- Negative self-talk

Negative self-talk is another part of your internal narrative about yourself, but it might sound like: 'It wasn't the outcome I'd hoped for because I messed everything up, I'm such a failure – this stuff always happens to me.'

This is probably obvious, but research shows over and over that people who regularly engage in positive self-talk have the greatest chance of success in all areas of life.

Negative self-talk is facilitated and perpetuated by our **cognitive distortions** – these are our habitual ways of thinking that are inaccurate and negatively biased.[11] These tendencies of thought form during adverse or stressful life events and are generally useful at the time to navigate that event. However, they are not rational or healthy thought patterns to maintain long term and only serve to keep us feeling bad about ourselves. We all engage in negative self-talk and we all have cognitive distortions, but we can improve this, leaving more space for productive and positive internal dialogues. When you become aware of that little voice in your head spouting negativity, keep an eye peeled for one or more of these distortions at play. Left unattended these distortions increase anxiety, deepen depression and cause problems in our relationships and a whole array of other unwanted frustrations.

THE TEN MOST COMMON COGNITIVE DISTORTIONS

○ Filtering

This involves ignoring, overlooking or actively explaining away positive aspects of an event to focus exclusively on the negative. For example, you deliver a presentation at work. At the end you receive a round of applause and some compliments from your colleagues on a job well done. However, on reviewing your feedback forms later in the day, you find one with a poor rating and a critical comment. This single piece of negative feedback overshadows every positive. It is what stays at the forefront of your mind when you recall the presentation and it becomes the catalyst for negative self-talk – 'that was a rubbish presentation' or 'I knew I did a terrible job'.

∘ Black and white thinking

This means habitually thinking in extremes or polarities: saying unrealistic and unhelpful things like 'I'm doomed' or 'I'm a failure', or seeing others as either good or bad, when the reality almost always exists somewhere in the grey area. This distortion is the same as **splitting**, which we looked at as a defence mechanism on page 60. People who use splitting to cope with conflict will likely use black and white thinking as their distorted self-talk.

∘ Overgeneralisation

This happens when we reach a conclusion about one event and then incorrectly apply that conclusion across the board. For example, you fail one business exam and conclude that you're useless at the subject in general. You have one bad relationship and conclude that all your relationships will be like that or that you are just terrible at relationships in general.

∘ Catastrophising

This is assuming the worst when faced with uncertainty. As we know, we hate uncertainty – it causes us great stress. So one way of resolving that uncertainty is to catastrophise an outcome. People who have developed this distortion have often experienced repeated adverse events, like chronic pain or childhood trauma. So those with a higher ACE score (page 22) may be prone to this distortion.

○ Personalisation

This means taking things personally when they're not connected to us or caused by us. This could be blaming ourselves for circumstances that aren't our fault or that fall beyond our control, or incorrectly assuming that we've been intentionally excluded or targeted. This is by far the most common distortion in thinking and something we have already touched on in both Chapter 4, 'Managing Intense Emotions', and Chapter 5, 'Understanding and Handling Stress'. Personalising things creates unnecessary upset, stress and negative self-talk. Simply decide 'I don't take anything personally' and your life will become instantly improved!

○ Mind-reading

This is assuming you know what others are thinking. The line between mind-reading and empathy (or intuition) can get blurred. One way to distinguish between the two is to simply consider all the evidence. Does the evidence confirm the thought or feeling? If so, you've tapped into empathy or intuition. If not, you're likely mind-reading or making assumptions. At this point it's best to resolve the assumption with open and honest communication.

○ 'I should' or 'I have to' statements

Mental chatter that tells you that you 'should' or 'have to' is a good reason to stop and assess for distortion. If these are not truly reasonable or self-motivational inner dialogues, they are negative self-talk – often rooted in internalised expectations from our family, society or culture. These expectations may not be supportive or appropriate for us as individuals, instead chastising us and bolstering a negative self-image.

○ Emotional reasoning

Another very common distortion – and something we covered extensively in Chapter 4, 'Managing Intense Emotions' – this is the false belief that our emotions are the truth or that the way we feel is a reliable indicator of reality. For example, you feel lonely so you surmise that no one cares about you, that your feeling surely confirms your unlovability. Or you feel overwhelmed by something and simply having such a feeling somehow 'proves' that you are incapable of handling the present circumstances. Emotional reasoning might sound like '*I feel* inadequate, so *I am* worthless.' Our emotions absolutely deserve to be recognised, validated and, if necessary, appropriately expressed. However, it's equally important to recognise that they are just our emotions. They do not need to disconnect us from the many alternative perceptions available to us in reality.

○ Labelling

This means reducing ourselves or others to a single, usually negative, characteristic or descriptor, or defining ourselves or others by a single event or behaviour. For example, we might describe someone as 'a drunk' or ourselves as 'a failure'. This is problematic for obvious reasons: no one is this uncomplicated!

○ Always being right

This distortion is what might result in observable perfectionistic tendencies or, on the other end of the scale, chronic imposter syndrome – it is the belief that we must always be right and correct. This distortion is strongly instilled in our schooling system and in many childhood homes. As an adult the idea of being wrong is absolutely unacceptable and reason enough to berate ourselves or defend our 'rightness' with the ferocity of an internet troll.

I've observed a **bonus distortion** in my own personal experience, possibly applicable to those who resonated with the freeze, faint or fawn stress responses in Chapter 3, 'Navigating Conflict'. When one of these three is our coping mechanism for the unpleasant feeling of anger, that anger more often than not turns inwards, fanning the flames of negative self-talk, habitual self-criticism and even self-loathing as a kind of crap release valve for the unexpressed emotion. Try to bring self-awareness to particularly cruel or unpleasant self-talk. Are you using yourself as a punchbag because it feels safer than processing or appropriately expressing your anger in reality or towards the person it's targeted at? Unacknowledged or suppressed anger, pent-up stress and certain unresolved conflicts are inciters and agitators of the most corrosive self-talk imaginable. The only cure, as with all emotional wounds and their nasty consequences, is recognition, validation, integration and, if necessary, appropriate expression.

Once we've brought our awareness of unhealthy and unhelpful negative self-talk by catching these common distortions, we can begin the work of reprogramming these thought patterns. We speak to ourselves more than we speak to anyone else – compare your self-talk with how you'd speak to a loved one. Do you think there might be room to show yourself a little more compassion? We can reframe our language and act ourselves into better self-talk with morning affirmations and reframing questions.

MORNING AFFIRMATIONS

> 'I figured that if I said it enough, I would convince the world that I really was the greatest'
> – MUHAMMAD ALI

Affirmations have become a bit of a buzz word in the (often confusing) world of wellness, so let me briefly explain how they work. The word affirmation comes from the Latin *affirmare*, which means 'to make steady or strengthen'. One of the key psychological theories behind positive affirmations is self-affirmation theory, the work of Claude Steele in 1988. Empirical studies have been done on the idea that we can use the uniquely human ability to produce language (internally and externally) to restructure and rewire the negative biases in our brains by affirming ourselves in positive ways.

The development of this theory led to neuroscientific research aimed at investigating whether we can see any real changes in brain structure when we use affirmations, and there is MRI evidence to show that certain neural pathways increase when we regularly self-affirm.[12] Well-established and widely accepted science exists to support this practice, but it's far from magic. Positive affirmations require regular use if we want to make lasting changes to the ways that we think and feel. Consistency, visualisation and making the affirmation visceral – really feeling it in your body as you think or say it aloud – is paramount. Also, according to self-affirmation theory, it's enormously important that your affirmations reflect your **core personal values and genuine strengths of character** – both of which we've established. Mindless, unconvincing repetition of something arbitrary that doesn't gel with what you believe to be good, moral and worthwhile will not get the upper hand on deeply engrained distortions of thought!

If you've read *Jump* you'll know that the affirmation most dear to me goes like this:

I am grateful,
I am pure love,
Love and light surrounds me,
Abundance unfolds before me,
Bliss is my default state.

I say that affirmation in my mind ten times the moment I wake every morning. But I also have many others written on little cards around my bedroom mirror. I just take what I need from this list when I need it and repeat it to myself as I go about preparing for my day. I will share them in the hope that some will be meaningful for you too:

- 'My life is abundant and full of joy.'
- 'Creative energy surges through me and leads me to new and brilliant ideas.'
- 'The more I focus my mind on the good, the more good comes into my life.'
- 'My capacity and potential are endless.'
- 'I am at peace with all that has happened, is happening, and will happen. I know it is for my ultimate good.'
- 'I believe in myself and trust my own wisdom.'
- 'I have something special to offer the world.'
- 'I radiate beauty, charm and grace.'

- 'I acknowledge my own self-worth – my confidence is soaring.'
- 'I accept and love myself, thoroughly and completely.'
- 'I work to help others and I possess the qualities needed to be extremely successful at whatever I choose to do.'
- 'I can accomplish anything I set my mind to. I am confident and capable.'
- 'My body is healthy, my mind is brilliant, my soul is peaceful.'
- 'I am happy, healthy, energetic and carefree.'
- 'I am gifted with and surrounded by amazing friends and family.'
- 'I am liberating myself from negative feelings and negative thoughts.'
- 'I am resilient, strong and brave. I trust myself to handle anything that comes my way.'
- 'My anxiety does not control my life. I do. I am safe, I am collected, I am calm. I return to my breath.'
- 'Wellness is the natural state of my body. I am in perfect health.'
- 'My future is an ideal projection of what I envision now. My efforts are being supported by the universe; my dreams manifest into reality before my eyes.'

Some other (more specific) affirmations to inspire you:

- 'My marriage is becoming stronger, deeper and more stable each day.'
- 'The perfect partner for me is coming into my life sooner than I expect.'
- 'My business is growing, expanding and thriving.'
- 'I deserve to be employed and paid well for my time, effort and ideas. Each day, I am closer to finding the perfect job for me.'
- 'Though these times are difficult, they are only a short phase of life. Change is coming and this will pass.'
- 'I forgive those who have hurt me in my past and peacefully detach from them.'
- 'I do not need to rely on others' judgement for acceptance.'
- 'A river of compassion washes away my anger, guilt or shame and replaces it with love.'
- 'Today, I abandon my old habits and take up new, more positive ones. I will only act in ways that are self-loving. I will give myself the respect and kindness I deserve in every single thing that I do.'

According to Ronald Alexander of the Open Mind Training Institute, writing your affirmations in a journal and practising them in the mirror every morning is a good way to make them more powerful and effective, so that's what we're going to do. Taking (and possibly editing) anything that has resonated with you from either of the affirmations lists above, and remembering to lean into your core personal values and strengths of character too, take some time to write your own list of morning affirmations.

_____

_____

_____

_____

_____

_____

_____

REFRAMING QUESTIONS

This is a very simple technique that transforms negative and self-limiting statements like 'I can't handle this!' or 'This is impossible!' into '*How* can I handle this?' or '*How* is this possible?' The former increase stress levels and stunt growth and problem-solving, while the latter do the opposite.

We can also use reframing questions at the other end of the day to our affirmations. At night, just before going to sleep, ask yourself these four questions:

- How am I so happy?
- How am I so successful?
- How do so many good things happen to me?
- How do I keep attracting such good people into my life?

Your subconscious mind will instinctively start to look for the answers to these questions and you'll start to see a shift in not only your self-talk but also your life.

Time to

ENGAGE IN SOME REFLECTIVE LETTER WRITING

If it feels right for you – and I really encourage this exercise – you may want to take the time to write a letter to yourself. Before you start, close your eyes, take a deep breath and bring to mind someone you deeply care for, respect and admire – maybe a loved one or a best friend. Feel the sense of safety, joy and compassion this person's presence generates in your mind, heart and body. Sit in that feeling for a few minutes. Imagine them smiling, imagine them truly, deeply happy and free from any suffering. Send them your unconditional love and feel their unconditional love in return. Try to stay in touch with this sense of joy, compassion and love as you write this letter to yourself. Forgive yourself for any time you've self-sabotaged or spoken words of self-loathing, for any time you've dimmed your own light, let yourself down, negatively distorted your own reality, perpetuated your own suffering or overlooked your wonderful strengths of character. As always, try to write in an unstructured, even ungrammatical, way and without judgement. Let the words flow from you as you show yourself deep regard.

_____

_____

_____

chapter 8
the science of awe and gratitude

'In every walk with nature one receives
far more than he seeks'
— JOHN MUIR

THE SCIENCE OF AWE

For as long as I can remember I've felt a strong and unwavering connection with the natural world. Even when I was very young, I think I understood innately that the wilderness is where we can find nurturing and wisdom – 'that the complex yet delicate riddles of its perfect synergy hold an intelligence far beyond our grasp', to quote a line from the pages of *Jump*. Throughout the couple of years I spent travelling the world in search of healing and meaning, the wilderness was the backdrop for every major lesson and Mother Nature herself the great egoless teacher. I have always turned to nature for perspective, strength and grounding, but I never understood why until very recently, when I discovered the work of Professor Dacher Keltner at the University of California, Berkeley.

Awe is an understudied yet potent – even life-changing – emotion, with profound benefits for wellbeing. A universal revolution in our understanding of awe began with Irish philosopher Edmund Burke. In his 18th-century masterpiece, *A Philosophical Enquiry into the Origin of Our Ideas of the Sublime and Beautiful*, Burke detailed how we feel the sublime (or awe) not only during religious ritual or in communion with God, but also in everyday perceptual experiences: hearing thunder, being moved by music, seeing repetitive patterns of light and dark. Awe was to be found in daily life, in obscurity, in the things that simply transcend our understanding. My first experience of awe is vividly described in Chapter 5 of *Jump*, 'My First Taste of Travel'. I was 19 and experiencing the emotion with such potency and frequency during a summer in Thailand that I began to call it my 'nature high'. A decade later the memory of that emotion would be the driving force in my decision to travel the world after burnout, seeking to re-experience its divinity and power in any corner of the globe.

I am now 32 and only beginning to fully cognitively untangle what my body seemed to recognise with ease – that cultivating experiences of awe in our lives, and bringing our full awareness to those experiences, produces physical and emotional wellbeing, stability and resilience. This is the essence of Professor Dacher Keltner's incredible work. He is the co-director of the Greater Good Science Center at the University of California, Berkeley, and his mission is to help people put social research, like this, to good use. His work has shown that about half the time we tap into awe from a social experience: like hearing a Martin Luther King speech or looking into our baby's eyes. But the other half of the time it comes from something in nature, and this single, transient experience can change who we are by rewiring our brains and bodies for the better. The data is truly striking. Simply spending time in the woods or in the ocean, walking with our bare feet on the earth, tuning into the trickling sounds of a stream, appreciating the leaves of a tree as they turn from green to yellow, watching the sun rise or set, gazing at the passing birds, clouds or sparkling stars of the night sky – all of these small acts equate to better physical, mental, emotional and social wellbeing.

On the purely social level, the awe we experience in nature humbles us. It offers a space and perspective that allows us to see ourselves in a new way. At the end of Keltner's research studies, participants asked more questions of others and spent less time thinking about themselves, they described themselves less arrogantly, reported feeling less entitled and self-important, and were less interested in material goods. Even brief experiences of awe appear to redefine our self-image and orient our actions towards the interests of the collective. I suppose it's simple, really: standing in the presence of vast or magnificent things – like a T. rex skeleton at a palaeontology museum or an expanse of giant oak trees – calls forth a modest, less egocentric self, which enables greater kindness towards ourselves and others.

However, growing up, our culture teaches us the opposite. The message reinforced is that we should be successful, achieve, and meet this or that expectation. We learn the gratification of self-interest very young – even if that interest has been bestowed upon us by someone else – and with every passing year our culture seems to be growing more individualistic, more narcissistic and more materialistic. So this idea of a sort of ego death can be uncomfortably at odds with a typical Western mindset. Could experiencing a dissolution of the 'self' be anxiety-producing? Isolating? Disempowering? Will it lower self-esteem? Keltner's research suggests that, in fact, we're still very much there, just minus all those unpleasant, nagging qualities of our conditioning. Awe takes us outside of our self. It stimulates wonder, curiosity and even innovative paradigm-shifting discoveries, like the work of Darwin or Einstein, whose awestruck desire to understand something new about our natural world changed it entirely.

Keltner's work is supported by Aleya Littleton, a trained therapist who specialises in **adventure and nature** as treatment modalities for mental health and wellbeing (I think I've just discovered my calling in life!). Her work monitors the effects of awe on a physical, mental and emotional level. Most notably, she has discovered that an increase in awe equals a dramatic increase in both vagus nerve activation and heart rate variability. These are two *monumental* markers of wellbeing in the body and mind.

○ The vagus nerve

The vagus nerve is the longest nerve in the body – *vagus* means 'to wander' in Latin. It originates in the brainstem and travels the whole way down our torso, touching the heart and lungs, snaking all around the digestive system and down into the lower abdomen, interacting with every major organ along the way. This nerve controls all our involuntary bodily processes and is a major player in the activation of that parasympathetic (or rest and digest) nervous system response that we covered in Chapter 5, 'Understanding and Handling Stress'. A healthy and activated vagus nerve means that everything from our blood pressure to our digestion to our orgasms is functioning optimally. It also allows us improved access to the parts of our brain responsible for creativity, leadership, emotional regulation and complex decision-making. High vagal tone marks a healthier nervous system and is associated with better mood, less anxiety and more resilience.

○ Heart rate variability

In healthy individuals, inhaling and exhaling produces steady, rhythmic fluctuations in the interval between heartbeats. In individuals who are unhealthy – mentally or physically – you see the opposite.

HEALTHY

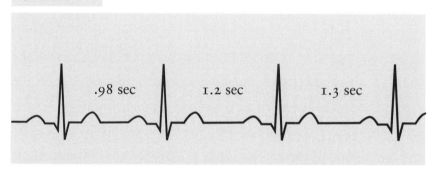

A healthy heart rate variability with variation between beats

UNHEALTHY

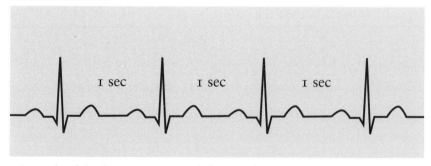

An unhealthy heart rate variability with constant intervals between beats

Heart rate variability is simply the pattern of the heartbeat, but it is also the tool through which we can gauge the health of our nervous system. The heart and the nervous system communicate with one another via the vagus nerve. Good heart rate variability is a measure of basic wellbeing. A strong, balanced nervous system gives us the ability to accurately respond to and recover from physical, mental and emotional stress. For example, individuals with good measurable heart rate variability will also display a reasonable degree of control over their response to frustrations and disappointments, enabling them to calmly assess what is going on when they feel, let's say, insulted or left out. They can choose how they want to respond and keep that response in line with their broader social intentions. Individuals with poor heart rate variability and, as a result, a poorly modulated nervous system are easily thrown off balance, mentally, physically and emotionally.

CULTIVATING MORE DAILY AWE

Awe certainly isn't the only pathway to increased wellbeing, but it's a *very* important and underutilised one – not to mention relatively effortless and inexpensive when you consider the implications for your quality of life. But beyond recognising the value of that weekend hike to that panoramic vista or the many benefits to be gained from an annual escape into the wild, how do we go about cultivating more awe in our day-to-day lives? It turns out that an emotion as big as awe can be found in the smallest of things. According to the research, it is a surprisingly common feature of our everyday lives, and taking some modest steps can have a major impact on our wellbeing. Don't underestimate the power of these simple suggestions for cultivating more daily awe:

- Spend less time working and commuting and more time outdoors or with other kind and uplifting people – even better if they're the awe-inspiring type!

- Take an 'awe walk'. Leave your devices at home, disconnect, find a trail, woodland, lake, hill, field, park or treelined road nearby and walk with all your senses engaged. Be present and give your full attention to the sights, sounds, smells and sensations of the natural world around you – again, even better if you can do this at sunrise or sunset, two especially awe-inspiring times of the day.

- Make a promise to yourself to look up from your phone more often and instead choose to fix your gaze on the beauty of the natural world around you, even if it's the butterflies, birds, greenery, clouds or other elements of nature we can find in a busy urban setting. Nature is everywhere when we decide to look for it.

- Attend an arts event – live music, theatre, museums and galleries often make the hairs on the back of our neck stand up.

- Seek out experiences that give you goose bumps and nurture your own hunger for awe. Take the time to pause and open your mind to those things which you do not fully understand.

I hope I have convinced you that awe is an incredible emotion to tap into as often as you can as you go about your daily life. To start cultivating some awe right now, take a few minutes to work through these questions.

Journal prompts
TO START CULTIVATING AWE RIGHT NOW

If you could design every minute of it from start to finish, what would a great day look like to you?

_____

_____

_____

_____

_____

_____

_____

_____

_____

_____

What is meaningful to you?

_____

_____

_____

_____

_____

_____

_____

_____

_____

_____

Who is meaningful to you?

_____

_____

_____

_____

_____

_____

_____

_____

_____

_____

What ignites your sense of joy?

_____

_____

_____

_____

_____

_____

_____

_____

_____

_____

_____

What makes you smile/laugh?

_____

_____

_____

_____

_____

_____

_____

_____

_____

_____

_____

How would you define your purpose?

_____

_____

_____

_____

_____

_____

_____

_____

_____

_____

_____

What feeds your soul?

_____

_____

_____

_____

_____

_____

_____

_____

_____

_____

_____

_____

What is the belief you hold most dear?

_____

_____

_____

_____

_____

_____

_____

_____

_____

_____

_____

_____

_____

_____

_____

_____

_____

_____

On completion, you could refer back to your core personal values on page 146 to see if your answers for cultivating awe are in alignment with your answers for what matters most to you. This could be an interesting piece of self-reflective work if you spot any incongruencies between the two.

'You will lose everything. Your money, your power, your fame, your success, perhaps even your memories. Your looks will go. Loved ones will die. Your body will fall apart. Everything that seems permanent is impermanent and will be smashed. The experience will gradually, or not so gradually, strip away everything that it can strip away. Waking up means facing this reality with open eyes and no longer turning away. But right now, we stand on sacred and holy ground, for that which will be lost has not yet been lost, and realising this is the key to unspeakable joy. Whoever or whatever is in your life right now has not yet been taken away from you. This may sound trivial, obvious, like nothing, but really it is the key to everything, the why and how and wherefore of existence. Impermanence has already rendered everything and everyone around you so deeply holy and significant and worthy of your heartbreaking gratitude. Loss has already transfigured your life into an altar.'

– JEFF FOSTER

Hundreds of studies have been done over the last decade on the practice of gratitude and the general consensus is this: those who consciously count their blessings are happier, healthier and more satisfied with their life. Robert Emmons is perhaps the world's leading scientific expert on the topic and he describes gratitude in two parts. First, 'it's an affirmation of goodness. We affirm that there are good things in the world, gifts and benefits we've received.' And second, 'we recognize that the sources of this goodness are outside of ourselves ... We acknowledge that other people – or even higher powers, if you're of a spiritual mindset – gave us many gifts, big and small, to help us achieve the goodness in our lives.'[13] According to Emmons, this social dimension is especially important to gratitude. It encourages us not only to appreciate the people and things around us, but also to repay or pay forward those gifts, and altruistic giving of any kind is chicken soup for the soul. The mindful practice of gratitude creates a kind of infinite feel-good feedback loop of receiving and giving, and giving and receiving.

We spend so much of our time and energy pursuing the things we do not have. The practice of gratitude momentarily reverses our priorities and helps us to appreciate the people and things we do have, with lasting and impressive benefits like these, which were identified in studies by Robert Emmons and his colleagues:

- A measurable reduction in anxiety and depression, even marked in those coping with chronic illness or pain

- A measurable increase in the strength of immune function and blood pressure, alongside a decrease in pain perception

- A measurable improvement in sleep quality

- A measurable increase in resilience, so much so that the practice is now used as an additional tool alongside therapy for suffers of PTSD, including war veterans

- A measurable improvement in the quality and satisfaction of our personal relationships – and healthy, functioning personal relationships are one of the universal markers of a long and happy life

- A measurable increase in the tendency to practise forgiveness, relieving us of the burdens of unresolved anger, hatred or resentment

- A measurable decrease in rumination on negative experiences and emotions

- A measurable and lasting effect on the brain, which trains the brain to be more sensitive to gratitude over time

We can all develop the skills of gratitude and reap the benefits. Those benefits are not immediate – studies show they take about four weeks to become noticeable in brain scans. But by week 12 they have increased measurably and then continue to increase over time. This is quite incredible, as most other positive activities start to see a *decrease* in benefits over time, with thanks to habituation. However, that infinite feel-good feedback loop gives the practice of gratitude a uniquely positive snowball effect!

CULTIVATING MORE DAILY GRATITUDE

Here are some specific, science-based exercises to help you to cultivate a powerful attitude of gratitude. They're from the Greater Good Science Center of UC Berkeley and its Greater Good in Action programme, which provides science-based practices for a meaningful life. Choose whichever exercise (or selection of exercises) you like best and try to incorporate it/them into your day for a minimum of four weeks to begin to reap the rewards and, hopefully, make this a lasting habit.

Three good things

Each day, write down three things that went well for you that day and provide an explanation for why they went well. It's important to create a physical record by writing them down – it is not enough to simply do this exercise in your head. The items can be relatively small in importance ('my co-worker made the coffee today') or relatively large ('I earned a big promotion'). To make this exercise part of your daily routine, writing before bed is helpful.

As you write, follow these steps:

- Give the event a title (for example, 'my co-worker made the coffee today').
- Write down exactly what happened in as much detail as possible, including what you did or said and, if others were involved, what they did or said.
- Include how this event made you feel at the time.
- Add how this event made you feel later (including now, as you remember it).
- Explain what you think caused this event – why it came to pass.

Use whatever writing style you like, and don't worry about perfect grammar and spelling. Use as much detail as you like.

If you find yourself focusing on negative feelings, refocus your mind on the good event and the positive feelings that came with it. This can take effort but gets easier with practice and can make a real difference to how you feel.

Call to mind someone who did something for you for which you are extremely grateful but to whom you never expressed your deep gratitude. This could be a relative, friend, teacher or colleague. It may be most helpful to select a person or act that you haven't thought about for a while – something that isn't always on your mind. Now, write a letter to that person, guided by the following steps:

- Write as though you are addressing this person directly ('Dear _____').
- Don't worry about perfect grammar or spelling.
- Describe in specific terms what this person did, why you are grateful to them and how this person's behaviour affected your life. Try to be as concrete as possible.
- Describe what you are doing in your life now and how you often remember their efforts.
- Try to keep your letter to roughly one page (approximately 300 words).
- Try, if at all possible, to deliver your letter to this person – there are some truly amazing and reciprocal benefits in having your gratitude received. However, this is totally optional, and you will enjoy the benefits of your gratitude practice even if you don't share your words.

○ Mental subtraction of positive events

Here's how to appreciate what you have by imagining your life without it.

- Take a moment to think about a positive event in your life, such as an academic or career achievement, the birth of a baby or a special trip you took – anything at all that comes to mind.
- Think back to the time of this event and the circumstances that made it possible.
- Consider how this event might never have happened – for example, if you hadn't heard about a job opening at the right moment.
- Write down all the possible events and decisions – large and small – that could have gone differently and prevented this event occurring.
- Imagine what your life would be like now if you hadn't enjoyed this positive event and all that flowed from it.
- Shift your focus to remind yourself that this event actually did happen and reflect on the benefits it has brought you. Now that you have considered how things might have turned out differently, appreciate that these benefits were not inevitable in your life. Allow yourself to feel grateful that things happened as they did.
- You can also adapt this practice to become the mental subtraction of a relationship and take the same steps to appreciate a loved one by imagining your life without them.

° Give it up

Learn how to truly savour with this trick to bring you lasting happiness. See if you can give up a different pleasure for one week each month.

- Select something that you enjoy doing on a regular basis and that you have unlimited or nearly unlimited access to. A good choice may be a particular food or drink that you enjoy, maybe chocolate or beer.

- On day one, allow yourself to indulge as you normally would in this activity. Enjoy the chocolate bar. Pour yourself a glass of beer. Veg out in front of the TV.

- Then, for one week, do not allow yourself to indulge in this pleasure at all. If you're giving up chocolate, abstain from any foods that contain it. If you're giving up TV, try not to even watch a video on your phone.

- At the end of the week, allow yourself to indulge again. As you do so, pay attention to how you feel. Are you noticing certain physical sensations (for example, the taste and texture of the chocolate) more than usual? How pleasurable is the experience? What kind of mood are you in?

- Try to go through this same process with a different pleasure the following month. And in between these weeks of abstinence, try to focus your attention on the pleasures you enjoy every day. What are the activities or experiences that you actually enjoy doing? What do you enjoy about them – how do they make you feel? How do you think you would feel if you were prevented from enjoying these activities ever again?

This is one of my favourite exercises in gratitude, and a sense of joy and appreciation I discovered with vigour after having to fast for seven whole days to help heal my gut from an Indonesian parasite!

LIVING GRATEFULLY

I know it sounds a little morbid, but the quote on page 198 is one of my favourites, which I sometimes simply distil down to the mantra 'you'll be dead one day'. Maybe I'm alone in this, but getting metaphysical and focusing on the fleeting nature of my own life – the undeniable and impending fact of my mortality – makes me grateful for the simplest things every day and brings an awareness to how precious, delicate and momentary all of this is. I'll leave you with a final list of (again, science-based) reasons why it's truly better to live gratefully:

- Grateful people, on average, give 20 per cent more time and money to charity.

- Grateful people have stronger social connections and community bonds – which leads to a whole host of other health and wellness benefits cultivated by our prosocial relationships!

- Grateful people are happier people, and happy people's income is roughly 7 per cent higher (probably as a result of things like enthusiasm, cooperation, likeability and other related factors).

- The effects really are lasting and incremental. For every decade in age, gratitude was shown to increase by 5 per cent – that's one happy later life!

- Grateful people have 10 per cent less stress-related illness and are more physically fit and healthy.

- Overall the practice of positive emotions has been shown to add up to *7 years* to your life!

chapter 9
love and relationships

'The greatest happiness of life is the conviction
that we are loved; loved for ourselves, or rather,
loved in spite of ourselves.'

— VICTOR HUGO

As I sit down to write this chapter I am laughing a little
to myself. The immensity of love and the complexity of
romantic relationships is not something I have any particular
expertise in. In my 32 years I have had three significant relationships, all of which have run their – very meaningful but
equally agonising – course to separation. I don't believe that
the length of a relationship is equal to the weight of its value
or impact, or that its ending signifies that it was a failure. But
I certainly cannot preach to you about the rights and wrongs
or shoulds and shouldn'ts from any kind of position of success

according to society's standards. I'm still navigating my own way through love's muddy waters, the many disappointments of dating apps and the lingering baggage of relationships past.

THE FINE ART OF ATTRACTING A SUITABLE PARTNER

When trying to decide which aspect of this huge and universally important topic to focus on, I considered the maddening, all-consuming experience of heartache, which is something I have a lengthy and thorough knowledge of. Or maybe the consistent and conscious consideration, learning and compromise necessary to maintain even the most magical of unions over a lifetime – based on the literature rather than my personal accomplishment of such a feat, of course. But in the end I decided to stick to the niche most authentic to my own truth at this time: the fine art of attracting one's most suitable partner. The 'how to' for getting to enjoy that great happiness of life: the conviction that we are loved, utterly, wholly, completely loved, exactly as we are – something that is becoming increasingly rare in our new world of dating apps, with the promise and allure of something better always just a click away. Having now read eight chapters of this workbook, you won't be surprised that this is something we will attend to with tools of self-reflection, self-acceptance and uncompromising self-love. This means utterly, wholly and completely valuing our own worth and not settling for anything less than we deserve and want. This is an interesting and revealing area of personal exploration whether you, like me, are single or happily (or unhappily) coupled up.

I would encourage everyone, at every stage of commitment, to work through this chapter. Regardless of the angle from which I approach it, there are insights to be uncovered here for all. So, with our anchor dropped into the choppy waters of love and relationships, let's begin.

∘ There is no such thing as 'the one'

There are many people for every person, always. Our romantic partners are our teachers and our mirrors. And even in our most compelling experience of having found 'the one', once the swell of hormones and other intoxicating brain chemistry balance out after the six months to two years of bliss, we are going to at times be faced with that mirror: the real and flawed human who can show us all the ways we need to grow and develop. This is an unavoidable truth when it comes to intimate relationships. It is not always effortless, easy and conflict-free.

∘ Our relationships will reveal our early life traumas

We can choose to process our early life traumas, or we can wait for our romantic relationships to reveal them. Either way, they are coming out. And romantic relationships are unique in their ability to bring out the absolute best and the *absolute worst* in us. Nothing else in this world will bring you as undeniably face-to-face with the vulnerable, wounded, scared, unhealed, broken or destructive parts of yourself.

In Chapter 1, 'Early Childhood Experience and Attachment Theory', we learned that traumas do not need to be major life events. Not feeling seen or heard can be traumatic. A sense of helplessness can be traumatic. Being told you can't or shouldn't experience certain emotions can be traumatic. Having a parent who focused on appearance or made you feel lovable mainly for attainments or achievements can be traumatic. Having a parent who could not or cannot emotionally regulate or attune can be traumatic. Having your reality denied can be traumatic. We have to first rework our understanding of trauma to work on the things that trigger us most in our relationships.

- *Everyone* attracts their romantic partners using the attachment style conditioned in childhood

We examined this in Chapter 1. Why do we find one person attractive and not another? We can tell ourselves *lots* of stories to answer this question but the truth is we are subconsciously drawn to our partners because they fit the model of the love dynamics we witnessed growing up. When I say 'fit', I don't necessarily mean that they behave in the same way. It's more likely that they unconsciously mirror to us our own unmet capacity in one or more areas. We recognise in them aspects of ourselves that have been denied or that we have yet to integrate. As such, this attraction we feel is partly due to the invitation to grow into our potential alongside this person.

Taking this a step further, have you ever met someone and it felt like an instant addiction? Love at first sight? Everything you've ever dreamed of? Like you've known them your whole life after a single shared afternoon? This is the intense experience commonly known as trauma bonding – the unconscious recognition that this person's trauma fits your trauma, and vice versa. Your subconscious mind has identified this person as having many of the negative characteristics of your parent or parents combined. The implicit messaging here is 'this time I'm going to get it right'. There is a strong (unconscious) promise of healing in this union. But the fact is that we simply love to repeat what we know, even if it's not good for us. This person feels like your missing puzzle piece because, again subconsciously, you both believe that you will make each other whole. They feel like a soulmate because they can help you work out unfinished business from childhood. When we are magnetically drawn to someone, this is the reason. It is the work of our emotional brain and our nervous system, not our heart. We seek out these reenactments not only because there is the possibility of resolution but also because they replicate the extreme arousal of our fight, flight or freeze response, which is associated with a massive release of endorphins – even dissociation and numbness feel good! A variation of this scenario is when one person feels an instant firework attraction but the other person doesn't reciprocate. This happens when they represent the other half of your trauma, but you don't represent the other half of theirs, or vice versa. If you find this approach to understanding love and attraction interesting, I highly recommend the book *Getting the Love You Want* by Harville Hendrix.

○ The unicorn union

The closest thing I've witnessed in reality to that Disney concept of 'the one' is when two people meet with that lustful, all-consuming intensity of a trauma bond *but* then develop that intense attraction into a conscious dynamic – which is two people absolutely committed to working on themselves and the relationship at a shared, same-paced evolution. This is what I like to call a unicorn relationship. Your trauma was in degrees of opposition to their trauma. You came together to unconsciously mirror back the healing that needed to take place in each of you individually and then did that work together! A real-life definition of true and aspirational love if ever I heard one.

Okay, satisfied that I have thoroughly butchered the idea of love at first sight and explained away any magic behind the powerful intuition that you and this bewitching other were souls destined to cross paths in the night, let's get clear on what we actually, authentically want, but first …

Bearing in mind any insights gained from exploring our first years of life in Chapter 1, 'Early Childhood Experience and Attachment Theory', here are some additional questions for you to consider and reflect upon at this point.

- When you were growing up, were you made to feel shame for *who you were* rather than how you behaved – meaning you experienced 'You're bad/bold' instead of 'That was bad/bold' language around reprimanding?

- Were certain expressions of emotion unwelcome/nipped in the bud/mocked or ridiculed in your house?
- Did you ever feel ignored, disliked or unloved by your caregiver(s)?
- Did you achieve a sense of love and security by 'doing' rather than simply 'being'?
- Was there an excess focus on your looks, physique, athletic ability, academic achievement?
- Were good communication, conflict management and emotional regulation modelled in your home? (If so, did you grow up in Utopia?)
- Did you develop any fears or insecurities around abandonment or loss during your childhood or adolescence?
- Did the relationship(s) you witnessed growing up feel toxic, stale or controlling?

To expand on the last point, if you answered yes, your developing emotional brain likely formed the belief that this will also be true for you in any romantic relationship you enter as an adult. If healthy relationships were not modelled during your upbringing, or if the modelling you witnessed represented shame, rejection, confinement, unhappiness or pain surrounding commitment; then you may have internalised a story of inferiority or unworthiness around love, or you may have unconsciously rejected wanting any commitment because similar shame, pain, abandonment, unhappiness or confinement could happen to you.

Time to

MINDFULLY SELF-REFLECT AND BRING AWARENESS TO OUR EXPERIENCE

Take a pause to journal on what is surfacing for you around those questions. Did you experience any resistance?

_____

_____

_____

_____

_____

_____

_____

_____

_____

_____

_____

_____

_____

_____

_____

_____

_____

_____

_____

_____

DISCOVERING YOUR SELF-WORTH

Here we're going to acknowledge, in black and white, all the good things you bring to a relationship. Your intelligence, resilience, independence and accomplishments. Your uniqueness, your edge, your adventurous spirit. Your sunny disposition. Your commitment to self-development or your own betterment every day. Your kindness, empathy, integrity, loyalty, thoughtfulness or generosity. Your ability to really listen. Your creativity and passion. Your perky bum, great hair, smooth skin or bright eyes. Your love of the outdoors, music, fitness, fashion, astrology, horticulture – whatever! Your open-mindedness, your warmth, your circle of friends, your craic and banter. Why would you want to date you?

Tap into your inherent self-worth and acknowledge every single good thing you bring to the table in a relationship. If this list is not at least a page long you need to think harder.

_____

_____

_____

_____

_____

_____

_____

_____

_____

_____

_____

_____

_____

_____

_____

_____

_____

_____

_____

_____

Having really leaned into your self-worth and soaked in the many qualities that make you an absolute catch, I ask you to keep that sense of yourself at the forefront of your mind as we move into visualising and describing your authentic, whole-hearted desires in a partner. Try to completely detach from what you think you *should* want and write the truth of what actually lights you up. Let's pull away from ego ideas and deep dive into honesty, vulnerability and genuine self-discovery.

Pay attention to any self-limiting beliefs lurking here, attempting to hinder the fun and insight, trying to keep you thinking small or in line with conventional ideals that may not actually align with the core of who you are or what you want. The following prompts are adapted from the manifestation model curated by Lacy Phillips at To Be Magnetic.

Journal prompts

Describe your ideal partner at length – get really specific here.
What does he/she look like? What is his/her temperament
and personality like? How does he/she make you feel?

_____

_____

_____

_____

_____

_____

_____

_____

_____

Where do you two live? Again, feel into this – be descriptive
and specific.

_____

_____

_____

_____

_____

What do you two do for fun? What is it that you connect over?

_____

_____

_____

_____

_____

_____

How do you want to be treated by this partner?

_____

_____

_____

_____

_____

_____

What do the financials look like between you?

_____

_____

_____

_____

_____

_____

What is their career?

_____

_____

_____

_____

_____

_____

_____

What is their level of commitment to you and how is that expressed?

_____

_____

_____

_____

_____

_____

What is your day-to-day lifestyle like?

_____

_____

_____

_____

_____

_____

_____

How is the sexual exchange between you?

_____

_____

_____

_____

_____

_____

_____

What is their family like?

_____

_____

_____

_____

_____

_____

What are your shared goals and values?

_____

_____

_____

_____

_____

_____

As well as getting clear and specific on what exactly we want from a partner, descriptive journalling and visualisation like this also allow us to create a new relationship model in our mind. Like reprogramming our self-limiting beliefs, this allows us to begin to consider that such a relationship is possible. My advice is to step away from what you've written here, sleep on it and revisit it tomorrow with fresh eyes.

Re-examining the picture you've created of the relationship you most desire, it's time to distil the most important features into bullet points. Flesh out this list as much as possible based on your journal answers to the questions above. To offer a skeletal and generic example, your list could look like:

- *Dark eyes, light hair*
- *Emotionally available, trustworthy, funny, supportive, communicative*
- *We own a three-bedroom thatched cottage with ocean views in Wexford*
- *We share a love of travel and travel a lot together; we love to work out together*
- *Emotionally intelligent, loves and cherishes me, openly affectionate, quick to resolve conflict*
- *Creative, successful and fulfilled in their work*
- *We earn €150,000 together annually*
- *Family man/woman*
- *Aspires to marriage and children, is committed and willing to 'do the work' in a relationship*

- *Has a great relationship with their family and their family love me too*
- *We respect each other fully and have these shared values*

Now, being as specific and descriptive as possible, bullet point every one of the important features of your desired relationship below:

_____

_____

_____

_____

_____

_____

_____

_____

_____

_____

_____

_____

_____

_____

_____

_____

_____

_____

_____

_____

Now, for each bullet point on your list, let's reflect and go deeper by asking why this is important to you.

- Why do I want this?
- What does this attribute mean at the root?
- How does this attribute make me feel?
- Do I really want this? Or did I pick this up along the way as something I'm supposed to want?
- Am I seeking this attribute in another because I'm unfulfilled in myself?

Time to

MINDFULLY SELF-REFLECT AND BRING AWARENESS TO OUR EXPERIENCE

After refining the features of your desired relationship and examining why those particular features are important to you, take a moment to acknowledge whether any unworthiness came up for you during these exercises. At any point, were you telling yourself that you couldn't have this relationship in reality, and if so, can you tap into the underlying *why*?

_____

_____

_____

_____

_____

EXAMINING UNWORTHINESS

Do you know how many *years* I spent draining my own happiness with my brazen commitment to unworthiness? Too many. I would Instagram-stalk my ex daily, like a deranged masochist getting their hit every time he posted another lightning bolt emoji on some girl's photo – even better when I would witness this happen in the immediate hours to days after he would decide he 'wasn't ready' or 'able' for a relationship, again, three years into our relationship. I literally loved being led on. Inconsistency and unreliability mixed with some bad attempts at an apology and a sprinkle of good old-fashioned intermittent reinforcement (or a few irregular breadcrumbs of hope) was my cheat code for obsession. Waiting for him to stop stalling commitment and 'grow into' the relationship he told me he wanted was my favourite pastime, as well as making increasingly implausible excuses for his disrespectful or dispassionate behaviours.

Our brains are such confusing, complicated organs. We have to work so hard to learn the art of reframing or reappraisal when it comes to our emotional reactions to the things that concern us personally. But in our romantic relationships, we might *easily* reframe and reappraise away the issues for years on end. 'The poor thing – he's just so hurt, you know. He can't commit because he's so scared of the vulnerability of love, bless him!' and other similar tales of self-deception. I am *all* for living a life of gratitude, forgiveness and compassion for ourselves and others. But when it comes to our romantic relationships – which are an interpersonal exception to the rule of how we generally behave – we so often let ourselves down by committing to unworthiness, accepting too little, forgiving too much and practising compassion in one direction: away from ourselves. These are some commonplace examples of when we are *not* standing in our self-worth:

- Doing *anything* I did in that paragraph above – do not be like me!
- Dating or sleeping with someone you know you're just not into
- Waiting on someone to suddenly realise they truly love you and just couldn't imagine their life without you
- Investing much of your energy and hope in a fantasy where he/she becomes the person you want them to be, while denying the reality of who they truly are
- Staying in a union where your emotional needs are not being listened to or met with any genuine interest, support or care
- Willingly accepting less than you want and deserve, often while reframing what you have to make it acceptable to you
- Accepting someone taking advantage of you – leading you on, lying to you, manipulating you with false promises and conflicted actions, not respecting your feelings, passions, vulnerabilities, time, space,

boundaries, values or finances, and the list could go on
- Proceeding when you or they are still in another, unfinished relationship
- Attempting to fix or save someone who is committed to self-destruction, self-deceit, chaos or unhealthy attachment dynamics
- Staying stuck in the same uncomfortable, hurtful pattern for longer than you wish to remember – low self-worth loves to tell us this dynamic will change and so we stay, hoping and wishing and walking on eggshells

If any of the above resonate with you, you have three choices:

1. **Radical acceptance:** This doesn't mean you approve of (or are even particularly happy with) your reality, but you actively choose to accept it until you are willing or able to change it.
2. **Continued resistance (staying put in unworthiness):** This is your greatest source of dissonance and suffering, a tug-of-war between fantasy and reality. I do not recommend this choice. But bringing awareness to resistance can move us into the better choices of radical acceptance or change.
3. **Boundaries and change:** This is consciously deciding to change yourself, the things you can control and/or your environment. People with high self-worth practise boundaries easily and often.

SETTING BOUNDARIES IN OUR ROMANTIC RELATIONSHIPS

Setting and honouring our own values-based boundaries can be an incredible catalyst for change. Boundaries in your romantic relationship could sound like:[14]

- 'I won't accept being lied to.'
- 'I won't accept someone not doing what they say they will do.'
- 'I won't accept someone not willing to compromise and self-reflect.'
- 'I won't accept someone who behaves unacceptably with other women/men.'
- 'I won't accept someone being uninterested in my life.'
- 'I won't accept someone not respecting my feelings.'
- 'I won't accept someone who doesn't make me feel secure.'
- 'I won't accept bad conflict management.'

Moving from behaviours of low self-worth (self-betrayal, people pleasing, pathological altruism) to behaviours of high self-worth (setting and holding boundaries, saying no, putting yourself and your own wellbeing first) can be quite distressing and often elicits feelings of shame, guilt and self-blame. A simple but effective way to start to move into high self-worth behaviours is to ask yourself: 'What do I need to do to care for myself in this situation?'

Journal prompts

FOR DISCOVERING THE ORIGINS OF OUR LOW
SELF-WORTH

We're going to attempt to peel back the layers to find the origin
of some of our low self-worth in our romantic dynamics.

Write down the names of every significant relationship
you've had, even if it was without conventional labels: list
every person who was meaningful or impactful to you romantically. A one-night stand with a nameless silhouette is worth
noting if it genuinely mattered to you. Beside each name write
anything that happened in this dynamic that didn't make you
feel good. Any disrespectful behaviours, any time you weren't
seen or heard, any time your needs were disregarded or left
unmet. Make a note of how the overall tone of your feeling
was in this dynamic – did you feel loved, supported and happy?
Lonely, insecure and small? Or something in between?

_____

_____

_____

_____

_____

_____

_____

_____

_____

_____

_____

_____

_____

_____

_____

Reflecting on your list and the information on the dynamic beside each name, focus on the times you felt you were shrinking yourself, playing small, selling yourself short or walking on eggshells, the times you were not standing in your worth or upholding your boundaries. Do you notice any patterns around the 'where' and 'why' of these behaviours?

_____

_____

_____

_____

_____

_____

_____

_____

_____

_____

_____

Again, reflecting on your list and the information on the dynamic beside each name, what negative characteristics did your past partners have in common with your caregiver(s)? What did you feel you needed most from that partner? Was it what you may have also needed most from your caregiver?

_____

_____

_____

_____

_____

_____

_____

_____

_____

_____

_____

_____

_____

_____

No relationship is a failure: every relationship is your mirror and every partner is your teacher. If you can look back at your previous relationships and pinpoint the lessons gained from each experience, then every one of them can be considered a success. What growth and learning did you take from your past partners?

_____

_____

_____

_____

_____

_____

_____

_____

_____

_____

_____

_____

_____

_____

Time to

MINDFULLY SELF-REFLECT AND BRING AWARENESS
TO OUR EXPERIENCE:

A few questions for you to consider here:

- Do you regularly and willingly invest in yourself?
- Can you say with honesty that you love and value yourself?
- If not, are you willing to commit to healing these two aspects of your self-worth?

WHEN TO WALK AWAY

A big part of learning how to attract our most suitable partner is learning when to walk away from an unsuitable one. If you are experiencing uncertainty in your relationship, you could consider working through these journal prompts in your own time to gain some clarity.

- Are you and your partner misaligned on spiritual, financial or family views? If there is a fracture in one or all of these areas it may be time to leave (or step up to that unicorn dynamic and do the work together in therapy).
- If none of these factors is at play, why do you want to leave the relationship?
- What is making you feel like you're not ready to leave? What parts of you do you believe will vanish with the relationship?
- Are fear and codependency at play?
- How is your attachment style factoring into this situation?

Anytime we leave behind what we know to be safe and step into the unknown, with only blind faith that something better is waiting for us, just beyond courage, is scary. So many people stay in unsatisfying relationships because it's more comfortable than feeling the awful pain of loss and loneliness. But we deserve to be in a relationship with someone we truly adore and who truly adores us in return. And we very often need to see, feel and heal the parts of ourselves that hurt most when we're alone.

The Kübler-Ross Change Curve

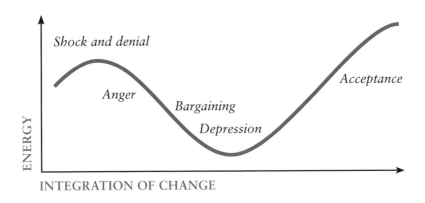

The Change Curve is based on a model originally developed in the 1960s by Elisabeth Kübler-Ross to explain the grieving process. It is normal to undulate up and down and back and forth along it, feeling all these emotions – shock, denial, anger, bargaining, depression, acceptance – for an undeterminable amount of time. But you can find reassurance in the fact that we are all quick to tell ourselves that it didn't work because we mustn't have been good enough or worth working for. We all convince ourselves that we will never find love again, that this person was the best we'll ever know, that we're destined to be alone for ever. But that is simply not true. Use the mantra 'If not this, then something better', and I promise you, if you're doing the work to raise your self-worth, it will *always* be something better – whether you ended the relationship or it was ended for you.

For those of you lucky enough to have found your best friend, your significant other, your twin flame, your soulmate, I would very much recommend *The Five Love Languages: How to Express Heartfelt Commitment to Your Mate* by Gary Chapman. This book has become something of a modern cult classic because the insights to be gained from it are impressive, especially for those committed to creating that unicorn relationship dynamic!

But homework aside, I'd like to introduce you to psychologist and clinician John Gottman, founder of the famed Gottman Institute, who has developed a research-based approached to relationships. He has spent his lengthy and impressive career working to predict divorce and marital stability with incredibly accurate results derived from longitudinal studies of couples. These studies have resulted in some compelling and universally applicable findings that may be of interest to you.

Conflict is inevitable in every relationship, but the difference between happy and unhappy couples is the balance between positive and negative interactions during conflict, and according to the research there is a very specific ratio that makes love last. That 'magic ratio' is 5 to 1. This means that for every negative interaction during conflict, a stable and happy couple has five (or more) positive interactions.

Negativity holds a great deal of emotional power, which is why it takes five positive interactions to overcome any one negative interaction. Negative interactions do happen in healthy relationships, but they are quickly repaired and replaced with validation and empathy.

POSITIVE INTERACTIONS

Below is a list of interactions that stable couples regularly use to maintain positivity and closeness:

- **Interest and attention to what your partner is saying:** expressed by asking open-ended questions or with body language like eye contact and nods.
- **Expressing affection:** self-explanatory.
- **Intentional appreciation and displays that they matter:** practising gratitude and appreciation for all of your partner's wonderful traits, showing that you care and that you are putting their interests on a par with your own.
- **Finding opportunities for agreement:** seeking an alliance in conflict.
- **Empathising and apologising:** offering genuine curiosity about and consideration of their perspective, and referring to our template on 'how to make proper amends' from Chapter 3, 'Navigating Conflict', to apologise for any hurts.
- **Accepting your partner's perspective:** this small shift, understanding that each of your perspectives are valid, even if they are opposed to each other, can drastically improve conflict.

- **Making (respectful and appropriately timed) jokes:** maybe even a cute inside joke that highlights the exclusivity between you. There is nothing like a little humour to lighten tension. Plus, life is short and love is a wonderful gift.

NEGATIVE INTERACTIONS

There are four negative communication styles that predict the end of a relationship. It is for every one of these types of interactions that we require those five positives.

○ Criticism

Unlike a critique or complaint, which is perfectly acceptable, this is an attack on your partner at the core of their character. It's really important to learn the difference between an expression of complaint and one of criticism. A complaint is spoken in 'I' terms: 'I felt', 'I thought', 'I was'. A criticism is spoken in 'you' terms: 'You never', 'You are', 'You did/do'. Being critical of each other not only leads to feelings of hurt and rejection but also paves the way for contempt, and contempt is a *big* problem in relationships!

○ Contempt

This is truly mean communication and the single biggest predictor of separation and divorce. Contempt involves disrespect, mocking with sarcasm, ridiculing, name-calling, mimicry or body language such as eye-rolling or scoffing. It is the most insidious behaviour possible in any normal relationship and needs to be actively eradicated by both partners if the relationship is to survive and thrive. Who knew a simple eye-roll could hold such predictive power and pain?

○ Defensiveness

It is perfectly understandable to defend yourself against unjust criticism, but it is harmful when defensiveness is used as a means of avoiding responsibility, admission of fault or taking the time to understand your partner's perspective. This communication style tells your partner that you don't take their concerns seriously and you are not willing to take responsibility for your mistakes. Defensiveness escalates conflict, as it is really a way to reverse the blame onto your partner in an attempt to make it their fault. This communication style can become almost omnipresent in relationships that are failing.

○ Stonewalling

This is when no communication is happening at all – rather than confronting the issues at hand, the listener withdraws from the interaction, shuts down and simply stops responding to their partner. This usually happens in response to contempt. It takes time for the negativity created by the first three negative communication styles to become overwhelming enough that stonewalling becomes an understandable 'out', but when it does, it frequently becomes a bad habit and isn't easy to stop. It happens when the body and mind become flooded and rational discussion is no longer within reach.

Time to

MINDFULLY SELF-REFLECT AND BRING AWARENESS TO OUR EXPERIENCE

This could be an interesting time to practise some reflection and self-awareness, evaluating your (current or past) relationship(s) in light of the research we have just covered. Do you engage regularly in positive interactions fostering empathy and closeness? Do you think you've mastered the magic ratio? Do you recognise any of the negative communication styles in your romantic dynamic? As always, bring your awareness to any resistance surfacing for you also.

_____

_____

_____

_____

_____

_____

_____

_____

_____

_____

_____

_____

_____

_____

_____

_____

_____

_____

_____

_____

_____

_____

_____

Time to

ENGAGE IN SOME REFLECTIVE LETTER WRITING

At this point (with so much more insight under your belt) you may want to revisit or rewrite the letters you wrote to your caregiver(s) at the end of Chapter 1, 'Early Childhood Experience and Attachment Theory', and/or to the people you addressed at the end of Chapter 3, 'Navigating Conflict'. Was one of those letters written to an ex? Do you have anything to add, retract, reframe or edit now as a result of your personal growth and improved self-awareness?

chapter 10

future-self journalling

'The best way to predict your future is to create it'
— ALAN KAY

As it implies, future-self journalling is the daily practice of intentionally and continuously creating a new, more fulfilling version of you. I was introduced to this brilliant practice through psychotherapist Dr Nicole LePera. It taps into our brain's incredible ability to change, restructure and rewire throughout our entire lives. This happens with thanks to neuroplasticity: we strengthen whatever we focus our attention on or whatever intentional acts we repeat. What begins as new and uncertain becomes natural and habitual as our brains grow new cells, form new connections and build new neural pathways to embed the thought pattern or behaviour, making it more automatic over time. I use this simple, quick writing practice every day for continual and consistent self-awareness and self-development.

Throughout this workbook we have been placing a spotlight on the autopilot habits, beliefs, feelings, behaviours and coping skills that we have been repeating daily in different areas of our lives since childhood, with a particular focus on the ones that no longer serve us. We have also been doing our best to address these weaknesses as we go. However, this is really the work of a lifetime, and I recommend future-self journalling as the tool you use to continue implementing changes and improvements as you see fit. This is also the tool you should use if you feel there is anything that you have highlighted in this workbook as a point of possible growth but have since left untended.

Our minds often don't know the difference between what is real and what is imagined and/or written, so mental rehearsal can quite literally make our dreams (and our dream versions of ourselves) come true. Writing or thinking in the present tense, 'I am', is training our brains that we have already arrived at the point of success that we hope to reach or achieve. This ritual is not a quick fix but it takes only 5–10 minutes per day and, with a little commitment, the pay-off is extraordinary!

There are five steps to future-self journalling.

1. Witness patterns of thoughts, feelings or behaviours that are keeping you 'stuck'

Now that you have worked your way through this workbook, step one is pretty much complete. We have already spent a lot of time self-witnessing and examining many areas of life – mental, physical, social, romantic, spiritual, financial and so on – bringing an awareness to the unconscious or habitual conditioning we might have in these areas. We have also worked through many options and tools to help us remedy unhealthy patterns in these areas.

So here you will consider what changes you can begin to make in each of these areas to bring you more fulfilment. Focus only on changes you can make yourself – you cannot control the behaviour of others. On the following page are some examples of how you might approach this.

2. Pick one small area of change

Keep it simple and **start small**. Too much change too quickly is overwhelming and unsustainable. Our bodies and minds love familiarity and the safety of what we've always known and done – even if it's not in our best interests!

Looking at the list you made in Step 1, which area feels most possible for you to change right now? Don't worry about what you pick to focus on first – there is no right or wrong. Just go with the one that feels most realistic and approachable for you at this time.

WHAT I HAVE WITNESSED	WHAT I CAN CHANGE
I often feel overreactive and not able to handle my emotions.	*I can practise a quick breath-work exercise followed by the RAIN technique to regulate my body's emotional reactions.*
I don't feel my needs are understood, met or honoured in relationships.	*I can practise becoming more aware of my wants and needs in relationships, and then actively move in the direction of radical acceptance or setting boundaries and change.*
I don't feel connected to my intuition and I struggle to know what's best for me.	*I can practise connecting to my physical body, where my intuition resides, through mindfulness practices like yoga and meditation. I can also lean into my strengths of character and core personal values.*
I feel pulled in many different directions as I try to start my day.	*I can practise mindfully creating a morning routine, starting my day with one small choice for myself.*
I find it difficult to say sorry in my professional/personal life.	*I can begin practising saying sorry, using the template in this workbook on how to make proper amends, to small things that don't cause me great emotional arousal.*

WHAT I HAVE WITNESSED	WHAT I CAN CHANGE

We want to make this manageable and lasting, so sticking with one small habit change at a time helps us to keep this daily promise to ourselves. Over time this builds to bigger and bigger changes as our self-confidence and self-trust grow.

3. Set the conscious intention to create change in that chosen area daily

Set aside a time each day when you have a little space, your mind is clear and you can tap into a peaceful state. There is no right time – it can be morning, midday or evening. The only caveat is that you don't do this exercise when you're stressed or feeling emotionally taxed.

Short daily journalling will probably be a new habit in itself, so once you have decided on a time in your day that works best for you, set an alarm or put a reminder in your phone to help you remember. Keep your journal in a space where it's convenient too.

If you do skip a day, don't stress – it's completely okay and very normal in the beginning. Try to avoid slipping into negative self-talk as a result ('I never finish what I start', 'I'm so lazy'). Affirm to yourself that you will start again tomorrow. With each new habit there are times when we will not show up. This is okay and a big part of the journey back to self-trust. Tomorrow is always a new opportunity.

4. Repeat consistently to create long-lasting change

Creating long-lasting changes to long-standing habits requires two things: your commitment and your ability to overcome the resistance you will experience around doing this new work. There is no quick fix. To rewire the brain we need to commit to this one area of habit creation for *at least* 30 days.

5. Use the daily journal prompts

Use the daily journal prompts at the back of this book.

Today, I am practising ... The ONE area you have committed to work on to create change.

Witnessing when I feel overreactive and not able to handle my emotions.

I am grateful for ... This simple gratitude practice helps to shift your energy on to the positive before getting to work on your new habit creation. Implement your favourite gratitude tool here from Chapter 8, 'The Science of Awe and Gratitude'. For example, here you could write your 'three good things'.

Today, I am ... Write and affirm your desired self/outcome/ thought or behaviour change in the present tense.

Calm, capable and clear-minded. I practise my quick breath-work exercise and the RAIN technique to regulate my body's emotional reactions.

Change in this area allows me to feel ... Habitual thoughts become habitual feelings. Note how you would begin to feel (about yourself, others, your world) if you began to believe in your new thought written above. Continue to write in the present tense here, as if it is already reality.

I am incredibly proud of how I handled that emotionally intense situation. What would have thrown off my whole day in the past is now something I navigate easily, with integrity and from a place of personal power.

Today, I am practising when … Note how and when you will be able to practise your change(s) throughout your day.

I notice my emotions starting to feel unstable or my mind under pressure. I use my awareness of these changes as a cue to pause and make different choices.

SOME USEFUL TIPS FOR YOUR FUTURE-SELF JOURNALLING PRACTICE

- Relieve yourself of any need for perfectionism and instead commit to doing your best every day. If you can only do one question, just do one question and build on this. The simple act of completing a task you've committed to, no matter how small, is incredibly healing. As self-trust and habit grow, your commitment will improve too.

- Remember to stay focused daily on **one area** of change for *at least* **30 days**. Repetition is key to forming new habits (and the neuronal pathways that go with these changes). Many of your entries may stay exactly the same for the full 30 days, or they may slightly evolve and change alongside your evolving and changing behaviour.

- Have **patience**. Change takes time and many of your new habits may take longer than 30 days to form. Stick with each area of change until you find it becoming more effortless and consistent. Make sure you witness this consistency before moving on to work on a new area.

- You will likely not believe your new present tense or 'I am' affirmations at first (and may not even feel truly grateful for the things you list). This is okay – again, there is no need for perfectionism. Just showing up, doing your best and trusting the process is enough. In time, with consistent practice, you will witness the change.

- Notice and celebrate your successes daily! Simply showing up to your journal practice deserves to be acknowledged. Don't let that inner critic minimise or invalidate your progress. Observe **any and all** personal changes as they slowly accumulate over time. This the fuel for self-motivation.

- And most important – remember, your ego (whose job it is to keep you repeating your old, familiar and safe habits and behaviours regardless of whether they serve you well) will likely get particularly grumpy and increase the levels of mental resistance around this daily task. That might involve a louder than usual inner critic, more pronounced negative self-talk or a diminishing of the value or progress to be found within this exercise. **This will pass** as the ego adjusts to your active creation of your new normal. Just keep showing up, keep journalling and keep celebrating your small daily wins.

- You can use this journal template over and over – throughout your entire lifetime if you want – to continuously tweak your subconscious mind and consciously create your future self. In this sense, our work together technically never ends!

POWER AND FREEDOM

'Blame yourself or blame no one'
– MARCUS AURELIUS

Throughout this workbook we have examined all the aspects of ourselves that keep us from being free and living authentically – the fears that run our lives and the behaviours we enact on repeat to avoid as much as possible having to experience or feel those fears. Whether it's rejection, abandonment, disapproval, loneliness or loss of control – therein lies the room for healing and personal growth. Every person carries with them their hurts and anxieties, and nobody copes with them perfectly. We all come with our share of wounds, big and little. We all have things we need to heal. It is a life's work made possible by self-awareness followed by consistent effort and action.

Studying human nature and the human mind has made me considerably more compassionate towards the inner worlds of others, but it has also made me a firm believer in one fact: **the most important step towards healing is taking 100 per cent ownership of your life.** That means taking absolute personal responsibility for your situation, your relationships, your actions and your choices: taking full responsibility for your reality as it is. This puts you back in control of your life and your happiness. It is no longer up to your partner, your parents, your job or anything else outside of you to be the source of your good feelings or worth. Without taking this step and holding ourselves accountable we cannot implement change or step into our personal power.

I used to wonder when the work would be done. When the healing would be complete. But I've learned that self-observation has to become a way of life and even then, when things get overwhelming, our old defences will always be close at hand. Our learning and growth are never finished. The goal is to develop a deep understanding of ourselves and to cultivate the mental and emotional skills that allow us to continue to feel and then cope better with those feelings. To live richer, more comprehensible and satisfying lives. And as we begin to notice personal change, there are ways to recognise that we are healing – we can observe in ourselves an increased sense of personal power and inner freedom. Personal power looks like:

- An ability to take action instead of telling yourself you're stuck or choiceless
- Trusting yourself to make assertive, values-based decisions
- Using conscious self-talk for empowerment and self-motivation
- No longer betraying yourself to please others
- Setting boundaries in unhealthy situations
- No longer blaming others for any aspect of your reality
- No longer needing validation from others to sustain your self-worth
- No longer needing approval from others for your authentic life choices
- No longer using unhelpful defences to avoid doing the work needed for personal growth
- No longer questioning when things are 'too good'

Inner freedom looks like:

- Taking the things that happen around you *far* less personally
- Being less reactive

- Engaging in less rumination, worry and negative self-talk
- Living a more authentic and fulfilled life
- More confidence and self-expression
- More freedom in your body
- An ability to love deeply and without fear

A FINAL WORD

> 'We're all just walking each other home'
> – RAM DASS

At the very beginning of this workbook I asked you to write down what it was you hoped to gain from these pages. I truly hope it has met your expectations and helped you to grow in ways you perhaps didn't even expect at the outset of this shared journey. I hope it has or will bring you to personal power and inner freedom. I hope it has expanded your self-understanding, your self-belief and your toolkit to create the life you authentically desire. I hope it has eroded some of the unconscious limitations and ego mind tricks that keep us all trapped in unnecessary suffering, playing small and selling ourselves short. I hope it has given you permission to be the person you wish to be rather than the person you feel you have to be. I hope it has made and continues to make you feel more capable, more fearless, more awestruck and more proud of who you truly are. I hope it allows you to stop living to satisfy the needs and wants of others and to start living to satisfy your own – this is where your magic resides. I hope it has helped you to tap into your strengths, your worth, your passions and your heart, and I hope you share these out into the world. I hope it has accompanied you in feeling the full spectrum of emotion, and I encourage you to continue to *really* feel – to cry until your eyes sting when you need to and laugh until your cheeks hurt as often as possible. I hope it makes you pause and pick your battles more wisely, coat your conflicts in kindness, more aware of the wounds we all carry, more aware that we're all doing our best, and strong enough to admit when you were wrong. I hope it's shown you that while you cannot change others you can certainly change yourself and the things around you. I hope it has encouraged you to listen more, to be receptive – there's infinite learning in this simple act. I hope it has challenged you to climb the tallest mountain and dive into the deepest depths to find yourself, and I hope your desire for self-awareness only grows. I hope it's made it clear that the ordinary can be extraordinary and that simple appreciation will make you richer than any other gain.

And lastly, a gentle reminder of my favourite mantra, you only have this one life and one day all of its promise and potential will be over. I truly hope you find the treasure in its ups and downs. I hope you recognise your own endless potential and the countless possibilities available to you in every precious awe-filled day.

Date: __ /__ /__
Today, I am practising
I am grateful for
Today, I am
Change in this area allows me to feel
Today, I am practising when

Date: __ /__ /__
Today, I am practising
I am grateful for
Today, I am
Change in this area allows me to feel
Today, I am practising when

Date: __ /__ /__
Today, I am practising
I am grateful for
Today, I am
Change in this area allows me to feel
Today, I am practising when

Date: __ /__ /__
Today, I am practising
I am grateful for
Today, I am
Change in this area allows me to feel
Today, I am practising when

Date: __ /__ /__
Today, I am practising
I am grateful for
Today, I am
Change in this area allows me to feel
Today, I am practising when

Date: __ /__ /__
Today, I am practising
I am grateful for
Today, I am
Change in this area allows me to feel
Today, I am practising when

Date: __ /__ /__

Today, I am practising

I am grateful for

Today, I am

Change in this area
allows me to feel

Today, I am practising when

Date: __ /__ /__

Today, I am practising

I am grateful for

Today, I am

Change in this area
allows me to feel

Today, I am practising when

Date: __ /__ /__

Today, I am practising

I am grateful for

Today, I am

Change in this area
allows me to feel

Today, I am practising when

Date: __ / __ / __	
Today, I am practising	
I am grateful for	
Today, I am	
Change in this area allows me to feel	
Today, I am practising when	

Date: __ / __ / __	
Today, I am practising	
I am grateful for	
Today, I am	
Change in this area allows me to feel	
Today, I am practising when	

Date: __ / __ / __	
Today, I am practising	
I am grateful for	
Today, I am	
Change in this area allows me to feel	
Today, I am practising when	

Date: __ / __ / __
Today, I am practising
I am grateful for
Today, I am
Change in this area allows me to feel
Today, I am practising when

Date: __ / __ / __
Today, I am practising
I am grateful for
Today, I am
Change in this area allows me to feel
Today, I am practising when

Date: __ / __ / __
Today, I am practising
I am grateful for
Today, I am
Change in this area allows me to feel
Today, I am practising when

Date: __ /__ /__
Today, I am practising
I am grateful for
Today, I am
Change in this area allows me to feel
Today, I am practising when

Date: __ /__ /__
Today, I am practising
I am grateful for
Today, I am
Change in this area allows me to feel
Today, I am practising when

Date: __ /__ /__
Today, I am practising
I am grateful for
Today, I am
Change in this area allows me to feel
Today, I am practising when

Date: __ /__ /__	
Today, I am practising	
I am grateful for	
Today, I am	
Change in this area allows me to feel	
Today, I am practising when	

Date: __ /__ /__	
Today, I am practising	
I am grateful for	
Today, I am	
Change in this area allows me to feel	
Today, I am practising when	

Date: __ /__ /__	
Today, I am practising	
I am grateful for	
Today, I am	
Change in this area allows me to feel	
Today, I am practising when	

Date: __ / __ / __
Today, I am practising
I am grateful for
Today, I am
Change in this area allows me to feel
Today, I am practising when

Date: __ / __ / __
Today, I am practising
I am grateful for
Today, I am
Change in this area allows me to feel
Today, I am practising when

Date: __ / __ / __
Today, I am practising
I am grateful for
Today, I am
Change in this area allows me to feel
Today, I am practising when

Date: __ /__ /__
Today, I am practising
I am grateful for
Today, I am
Change in this area allows me to feel
Today, I am practising when

Date: __ /__ /__
Today, I am practising
I am grateful for
Today, I am
Change in this area allows me to feel
Today, I am practising when

Date: __ /__ /__
Today, I am practising
I am grateful for
Today, I am
Change in this area allows me to feel
Today, I am practising when

Date: __ / __ / __

Today, I am practising

I am grateful for

Today, I am

Change in this area
allows me to feel

Today, I am practising when

Date: __ / __ / __

Today, I am practising

I am grateful for

Today, I am

Change in this area
allows me to feel

Today, I am practising when

Date: __ / __ / __

Today, I am practising

I am grateful for

Today, I am

Change in this area
allows me to feel

Today, I am practising when

Date: __ /__ /__
Today, I am practising
I am grateful for
Today, I am
Change in this area allows me to feel
Today, I am practising when

Date: __ /__ /__
Today, I am practising
I am grateful for
Today, I am
Change in this area allows me to feel
Today, I am practising when

Date: __ /__ /__
Today, I am practising
I am grateful for
Today, I am
Change in this area allows me to feel
Today, I am practising when

Date: __ /__ /__

Today, I am practising

I am grateful for

Today, I am

Change in this area
allows me to feel

Today, I am practising when

Date: __ /__ /__

Today, I am practising

I am grateful for

Today, I am

Change in this area
allows me to feel

Today, I am practising when

Date: __ /__ /__

Today, I am practising

I am grateful for

Today, I am

Change in this area
allows me to feel

Today, I am practising when

Date: __ /__ /__
Today, I am practising
I am grateful for
Today, I am
Change in this area allows me to feel
Today, I am practising when

Date: __ /__ /__
Today, I am practising
I am grateful for
Today, I am
Change in this area allows me to feel
Today, I am practising when

Date: __ /__ /__
Today, I am practising
I am grateful for
Today, I am
Change in this area allows me to feel
Today, I am practising when

Date: __ / __ / __

Today, I am practising

I am grateful for

Today, I am

Change in this area
allows me to feel

Today, I am practising when

Date: __ / __ / __

Today, I am practising

I am grateful for

Today, I am

Change in this area
allows me to feel

Today, I am practising when

Date: __ / __ / __

Today, I am practising

I am grateful for

Today, I am

Change in this area
allows me to feel

Today, I am practising when

acknowledgements

First and foremost, my sincerest love and gratitude to my eternally supportive family. Without you I quite literally could not have returned to college to learn the content on these pages. From the bottom of my heart, thank you for everything you do.

It is very surreal to be writing the final few lines of my second book and I'm incredibly grateful to Sarah and Faith for the motivation and encouragement, and to everyone at Gill Books who made this dream into reality again. I have never experienced anything like the passion, purpose and flow of writing about the topics I love most. Thank you for making this genuinely life-altering pursuit possible.

Thank you to my mentors and unspoken personal heroes, Dr Yvonne Barnes-Holmes, Ray McKiernan and Brian Pennie. Your enthusiasm for your work is both a gift and an inspiration, I am so grateful and privileged to learn from you, and I deeply appreciate your generosity of time and knowledge. Thank you to Dr Micheál O'Keeffe for the preliminary-stage proofread; your guidance and insights were truly invaluable and greatly appreciated.

And to you, the reader, thank you for picking up my book and investing your time and energy into reading my words. It is something I will never, ever take for granted – not a chance. I hope you found it worthwhile, valuable or enriching in some way, and I hope you can refer to these pages if and when you need to, maybe even across a lifetime!

notes

1. Vincent J. Felitti, Bob Anda et al., 'Relationship of Childhood Abuse and Household Dysfunction to Many of the Leading Causes of Death in Adults: The Adverse Childhood Experiences (ACE) Study', *American Journal of Preventive Medicine* 14.4, 1998, pp. 245–58.

2. Rachel Yehuda and Amy Lehrner, 'Intergenerational Transmission of Trauma Effects: Putative Role of Epigenetic Mechanisms', *World Psychiatry* 17.3, 2018, pp. 243–57.

3. 'The Challenges of Anxious-Avoidant Relationships', The School of Life. <www.theschooloflife.com/thebookoflife/the-challenges-of -anxious-avoidant-relationships>

4. Joseph Burgo, *Why Do I Do That? Psychological Defense Mechanisms and the Hidden Ways They Shape Our Lives*, New Rise Press, 2012, p. 20.

5. Burgo, p. 20.

6. Burgo, p. 21.

7. Scott Atran, Robert Axelrod and Richard Davis, 'Sacred Barriers to Conflict Resolution', *Science* 317.5841, 200, pp. 1039–40.

8. Elissa Epel, Jennifer Daubenmier et al., 'Can Meditation Slow Rate of Cellular Aging? Cognitive Stress, Mindfulness and Telomeres', *Annals of the New York Academy of Sciences* 1172.1, 2009, pp. 34–53. Britta K. Hölzel, James Carmody et al., 'Mindfulness Practice Leads to

Increases in Regional Brain Gray Matter Density', *Psychiatry Research: Neuroimaging* 191.1, 2011, pp. 36–43.

9. For more about somatic experiencing, see Peter Levine, *In an Unspoken Voice*, North Atlantic Books, 2010; Peter Levine, *Waking the Tiger*, North Atlantic Books, 2017; Robert Sapolsky, *Why Zebras Don't Get Ulcers*, St Martin's Press, 2004.

10. Gaétan Chevalier, Stephen T. Sinatra et al., 'Earthing: Health Implications of Reconnecting the Human Body to the Earth's Surface Electrons', *Journal of Environmental and Public Health*, 2012.

11. David Tod, James Hardy and Emily Oliver, 'Effects of Self-Talk: A Systematic Review', *Journal of Sport and Exercise Psychology* 33.5, 2011, pp. 666–87.

12. Emily B. Falk, Matthew Brook O'Donnell et al., 'Self-Affirmation Alters the Brain's Response to Health Messages and Subsequent Behavior Change', *Proceedings of the National Academy of Sciences* 112.7, 2015, pp. 1977–82. Christopher N. Cascio, Matthew Brook O'Donnell et al., 'Self-Affirmation Activates Brain Systems Associated with Self-Related Processing and Reward and is Reinforced by Future Orientation', *Social, Cognitive and Affective Neuroscience* 11.4, 2016, pp. 621–9.

13. Robert Emmons, 'Why Gratitude Is Good', *Greater Good Magazine*, 16 November 2010.

14. These are based on the work of emotional health advisor Roxie Nafousi at her Relationships Online Workshop. <https://roxienafousi.com/>